JAMIE

A Literacy Story

Diane Parker

Stenhouse Publishers

York, Maine

Stenhouse Publishers, 431 York Street, York, Maine 03909

Library of Congress Cataloging-in-Publication Data

Parker, Diane.
    Jamie : a literacy story / Diane Parker.
       p.   cm.
    Includes bibliographical references (p. 113)
    ISBN 1-57110-058-x (alk. paper)
      1. Language arts (Primary)—Hawaii—Oahu—Case studies.
2. Literacy—Hawaii—Oahu—Case studies.   3. Muscular dystrophy in children—Hawaii—Oahu—Case studies.   4. Panui, Jamie, d. 1994.
5. Physically handicapped children—United States—Biography.
6. Parker, Diane.   I. Title.
LB1529.U5P37   1997
372.6—dc21   96-53586
                                                          CIP

Cover and interior design by Ron Kosciak, *Dragonfly Design*
Cover photograph by the author; interior photographs by Diane Parker, Laurie Panui, and David Andrin
Typeset by Octal Publishing

Manufactured in the United States of America on acid-free paper

01 00 99 98 97 9 8 7 6 5 4 3 2 1

To Hoyt, Nani, and Jennifer, with love

Contents

Acknowledgments

Writing is often described as a solitary act, but to me nothing could be further from the truth. Mikhail Bakhtin, the Russian literary critic, said, "The word in language is half someone else's" (1981, p. 293). Writing, like all learning and communication, is a social construction. I may sit alone at the computer, but the thoughts and words that filter through me carry the echoes of countless other voices. Family, friends, colleagues, and authors are at the computer with me and I feel their presence when I write. I can't name them all in these short pages, but I want to acknowledge those who have most directly influenced my growth and my work on this manuscript.

I'll begin at the beginning. My parents, Alfred and Celia Fichman, instilled in me a love of the written word, through their example and their gift of time. From my earliest memories and throughout my childhood, they read to me and with me. Dad was the best storyteller I ever knew. He was never too busy or too tired when my sister, Alice, and I would ask him to tell us another story or to tell the same one over and over. Although he died when I was nine, I can still close my eyes and feel again my excitement and anticipation as I awaited the next story. His words are in my head and heart.

When I began to write my own stories, Mom kept notebooks and pencils by my bedside so I'd have supplies at hand when I woke up and wanted to record my thoughts before I forgot what they were. I laugh now when I read what I wrote at age five, but I am grateful for Mom's understanding that everything begins with first steps. Her encouragement made me want to keep writing.

In my first year of teaching, I discovered the fascinating world of children's language as I listened to my kindergarteners' wonderful expressions and definitions (my favorite: "an echo is a loud shadow"). That was the beginning of my search to know more about literacy. I'm thankful to my first class and to all the children I've taught and learned from since, including my own two daughters, from whom I've learned the most. They are the reason I love teaching.

I want to thank two of my former principals. George Nakasone gave me the opportunity to return to the classroom, and he began our school's mainstreaming effort because of his belief in equity and justice for all learners. But for him, I might never have met Jamie and her family. Glenn Honda trusted me to find my own way as a learner with my Primary 'Ohana (Hawaiian for *family*) class, allowing us to construct curriculum together and to build the richest of memories.

Betsy Brandt taught me about the history and issues surrounding assessment practices in our schools. As an evaluation specialist, she works tirelessly toward assessment reform and has inspired me to assume an active role in this effort. She has continuously encouraged my work and my writing.

We are fortunate when we work with compatible colleagues. We are doubly fortunate when we can also call these people our friends. There are many colleagues and friends who have helped me grow professionally. We share a similar philosophy, yet we accept and value our diversity. Although some of them may not have a direct connection with this book, the support I feel as we learn from and with each other has kept me going through even the most trying times. I especially want to thank Alana Aki, Carrie Kawamoto (thanks, Carrie, for encouraging me to write this book), Betsy Sagara, Lynn Yoshizaki, and the late Dianne Yoshizawa. They are proof that learning is indeed a social construction.

"It is not often that someone comes along who is a true friend . . ." (*Charlotte's Web*, p. 184). I need to reserve a special thank you for Elaine Yoshioka. She has been a valued friend, confidante, mentor, and study companion who constantly pushes my thinking, unfailingly encourages my writing, and helps me increase my knowledge and professional experience. Her humanity, integrity, and professionalism set an example for all who know her.

Many faculty members at the University of Hawai'i are also friends who have greatly impacted my learning. When I enrolled there as a returning student in 1988, Helen Slaughter didn't hesitate before allowing me into her already full language arts course. Her inclusive philosophy enabled me to begin my renewed journey of learning, and her thought-provoking class inspired me to continue. Tony Picard has been a mentor and research collaborator in mathematics education. He helped me see that I had classroom stories worth sharing, and he taught me how to shape those stories for a professional audience (thanks, Tony, for encouraging me to get a computer). I don't know if I would have been able to write this book if I hadn't written with Tony first. Joe Tobin helped me move into qualitative research so I could begin analyzing the mountains of data I'd been collecting. Joe also gave me encouragement and practical advice when it was time to send out my story. Neil Pateman helped me learn more about the social and political issues that affect both teachers and students and that certainly affected Jamie and her family. Beth Pateman is helping me grow in my new role as a mentor to preservice teachers. I am grateful for her expertise and her support. With Diane Stephens, I've studied more about the reading process and learned how to look more closely at the particulars of helping readers. Diane willingly read my manuscript, offered valuable suggestions, and helped me find a title when I had nearly given up hope of doing so. She also put me in touch with Philippa Stratton, the most thoughtful and excellent editor anyone could possibly have. It has been a great pleasure working with Philippa, and also with Tom Seavey and Martha Drury on the production of this book; even deadlines don't seem as stressful because the process has been so enjoyable.

Grace Angel and Patricia Suenaga enthusiastically supported my work on the manuscript, which coincided with their student-teaching semester in my class. I appreciate their understanding, especially on days when I may have been preoccupied with rough spots in the revisions. Grace also gave me valuable technical assistance when I was preparing my computer files for production.

I am extremely grateful to the entire Panui family, and especially to Lambert and Laurie, for their willingness to share their story and for their time and effort expended in the process. Without their commitment to this project, this book would not have been possible. I'm thankful to them and to all our Primary 'Ohana parents for their involvement in their children's education, which made a difference for all of us and made our 'Ohana year unforgettable.

Finally, though most importantly, I want to thank my husband, Hoyt, and our daughters, Nani and Jennifer, for their involvement with my students and for their encouragement of this book. Hoyt has been with me every step of the way, reading draft after draft and helping me make sure my words communicate what I meant to say. I am grateful for his patient understanding of my need to write and his steadfast belief that this story would be published. My family's love and support in this project and our journey through life together have enriched me beyond words.

Prologue

It is remarkable how people's lives intertwine. People move in and out of our world, affecting us as we affect them, and we often don't know it until we look back on what has happened. What amazes me is the exquisite timing of these moves, which help shape our growth and the course of our lives.

When I think of the people I've known and the events I've experienced, I often wonder, What if? What if I had not been at a certain place at a certain time? What if I had met this person earlier or later, or under different circumstances? It's the same when I think of Jamie Panui. I wonder how things might have been if we had met a few years earlier, and I marvel that things happened as they did.

Jamie Panui became part of my life on September 1, 1990, when she was enrolled in my kindergarten class. I didn't know it then, but we would be together for three wonderful years, through kindergarten and first and second grade, and she would enter my heart and the hearts of my family.

The school in which I teach is in a small town on O'ahu, Hawai'i. The population it serves is ethnically and socioeconomically diverse; the majority of students come from low-income housing projects. I enjoy the diversity and the accompanying challenge to look at every student as unique.

When Jamie became my student, I was radically restructuring my curriculum. I had returned to teaching a few years before, after many years as a full-time wife and mom. I was confused by some of the changes that had taken place during the years I had been away from the classroom. I was surprised to find a heavy emphasis on worksheets, drills, and testing, even with the youngest children. This was counter to everything I had learned in the past. My undergraduate and graduate school courses in the sixties had strongly emphasized the philosophy of John Dewey and greatly influenced my belief that teaching and learning should be active, social processes, with children learning by doing rather than by passively receiving information. The classrooms I experienced in those days reflected this belief, and raising my two daughters validated this philosophy for me even further.

But I thought that since I had been away from teaching so long, I must be out of step. I felt I needed to update my knowledge, so in 1988 I began taking university language arts courses to learn more about current research in the field. I was so enthralled when I found that others were asking the same questions I was (and even studying Dewey again!) that I immersed myself completely in my studies, wanting to find out more. That immersion eventually gave me the confidence to try to change my classroom practice.

I was working in a very traditional school; basal readers and workbooks were used from kindergarten through sixth grade. I didn't like our kindergarten workbook; I used it because it was "required." But as I incorporated more authentic reading and writing experiences into my curriculum, I began to resent the precious time the workbooks stole from each day. With the empowerment that comes from being informed, I asked and received my principal's permission to dispense with the workbooks so that I could focus on more meaningful ways to help my students. Jamie joined my class at the beginning of my second "basal-free" year, when I was beginning to explore new aspects of my search to understand and foster literacy in my classroom.

My studies continue and have expanded to other disciplines. I want to know so much more than I do. But as I reflect on my three years with Jamie, I realize more fully than ever how much she and her family taught me as we sought to understand together. I tell their story with my heartfelt appreciation for their participation and with my unceasing wonder at the power of literacy to transform lives.

Introducing Jamie

Jamie

Jamie wasn't supposed to be my student or even be at my school, since she lived in another school district. Her father, Lambert, worked as a carpenter for a construction company. Her mother, Laurie, had previously worked at various clerical jobs but had since chosen to remain at home full-time to care for her family. Her brother, Jarrett, was a fourth grader at their neighborhood school. But Jamie was confined to a wheelchair, and the school's administrator discouraged her parents from enrolling her there, saying that she would have difficulty getting to their second-floor library. Laurie and Lambert then decided to try our school, which was not too far away from their home and which they had heard was more accessible. They had no problem enrolling Jamie.

Jamie had spinal muscular atrophy, a form of muscular dystrophy. She could not walk or use her lower body or leg muscles. She could, however, use her upper body and arms, although she tired very easily because of the weak muscles and chronic respiratory problems associated with her illness.

Spinal muscular atrophy causes progressive curvature of the spine. One reason for Jamie's respiratory problems was this curvature, which placed undue pressure on her lungs. She had had some serious bouts with pneumonia when she was younger, and she was extremely susceptible to all sorts of infections. If she had even a slight cold, she had to remain at home for a week or more so that Laurie and Lambert could suction the mucus that collected in her lungs. This was extremely uncomfortable and often painful, but it was essential. If Jamie could avoid the complications of secondary infections during her early childhood, she would eventually be able to undergo the corrective spinal surgery that could increase her comfort and resistance.

Jamie's condition was diagnosed when she was eighteen months old, at which time she became entitled to various special-education services. Laurie and Lambert took advantage of the available developmental programs, which helped Jamie with her physical needs and gave them valuable information and support.

When Jamie was three, she became eligible for a special-education preschool class, in which she spent two years. She was happy to be in school, but her parents were beginning to sense a potential problem. Most of Jamie's classmates had severe learning disabilities; Jamie had a severe physical disability but was quite capable mentally. She was also highly verbal, but there were no peers who could interact appropriately with her. Laurie and Lambert realized that Jamie would need much greater intellectual challenges as she moved on in school. They had no disparaging views about the other students; it was simply that this class environment could not meet Jamie's needs. They therefore sought to enroll her in a regular kindergarten.

They were especially worried that others might not see Jamie as they did. Jamie could be stubbornly uncooperative when she felt particularly powerless. In the doctor's office, for example, she would deliberately stiffen her arm when asked to hold it out for an injection, and she would meet the medical staff's pleasant overtures with unfriendly silence.

Special-education status, in spite of all the services it brings, can be even more disempowering. Children who are in special education must be monitored and tested regularly under controlled situations, in accordance with federal law. Jamie resisted these tests fiercely during her preschool years, often refusing to respond to the examiners. This exasperated Laurie and Lambert, who wanted the testers to know Jamie's capabilities, but they couldn't budge Jamie. They'd ask her, "Why don't you answer? You know that," and she'd whisper, "Because I know they're testing me." Even when she was observed from behind a two-way mirror, she would tell her parents, "I know people are behind the glass," and refuse to comply.

It reached a point where Laurie and Lambert thought they might have to videotape Jamie performing certain tasks at home, just to prove she was able to do them. But Jamie's preschool teacher knew her well, had documented her accomplishments in class, and fully supported her parents' request for a regular-education placement.

Our school's special-education department chairperson came to my classroom to talk to me about Jamie in mid-August, as I was preparing for the children's September arrival. He gave me a summary of Jamie's background and showed me her photo. Almost apologetically, he asked if I would consider taking her into my class. I was puzzled that he felt he had to ask. I had been mainstreaming special-education students for several years, some with speech and hearing difficulties but most diagnosed with various forms of mental retardation. I had therefore been taking university special-education courses to become more informed about the research and philosophy guiding current efforts to help special-needs students in regular classrooms. My studies and experiences had made me a staunch advocate of mainstreaming because of its well-documented educational and social benefits (Madden and Slavin 1983; Lewis and Doorlag 1987).

It was hard for me to think of Jamie in the same category, though. As I thumbed through her file, it appeared that she was "normal" in every way except that she couldn't walk! I could see no justification for placing her in anything other than a regular classroom. I felt that as long as her physical safety could be assured, we could adapt to her needs, by trial and error if necessary. As a teacher, I've always believed that if a child is sent to me, there's a reason I'm supposed to work with that child. I didn't hesitate; I agreed to take Jamie. I didn't see it as a problem. And I thought, too, What if she were my child? Wouldn't I want her to have the same opportunity?

Laurie brought Jamie to school before classes officially began so that we could meet and Jamie could see her new classroom. I was surprised at how tiny and thin Jamie was. She wore a cute flowered lavender dress and shiny white shoes. Her dark eyes looked big in her small heart-shaped face framed with long black hair and bangs. She was a delicate, pretty composite of her Hawaiian-Japanese-Filipino-Chinese heritage. She was very quiet (her typical behavior in new situations), but she looked around the room with interest.

Laurie and I discussed initial procedures, agreeing that we would make needed changes as we went along. Either Laurie or Lambert would get Jamie to and from school each day, bringing her into the classroom in the morning and picking her up from there in the afternoon. This would also let us talk with each other every day, something we would almost certainly need to do, especially at the beginning.

Jamie would use three different chairs each day. One was her wheelchair, which was motorized and which she was able to operate proficiently. She also had a small wooden chair, just a few inches high, that Lambert had designed, which would enable her to participate at the same level as everyone else during the frequent times we would all gather on the floor. We had also ordered, from our state Department of Health, a customized chair that Jamie could use as she sat at a desk or table. Each chair provided her with the support she needed to be able to sit upright. I would need to lift and carry her from one chair to the other, which would be relatively easy because she was so small. Laurie assured me that Jamie could be lifted normally and that I wouldn't hurt her.

My one concern was for Jamie's physical safety. I hadn't yet met the other children who would be in our class and I didn't know how dependable they would be. Kindergarteners can be quite active and there are always a few who are rough. I knew it would be impossible for me to be with Jamie constantly, with twenty-one other children to attend to, and I was afraid that somehow Jamie might accidentally be tipped over in her wheelchair. Because the special-education department shared that concern, they assigned an aide to stay with Jamie in our classroom. The aide would also take her to the bathroom and the cafeteria. That arrangement seemed satisfactory. And Laurie would accompany us on all our field trips.

Laurie and Lambert had another concern, however. Although they hoped Jamie would progress academically, their main goal for her kindergarten year was for her to have the opportunity to interact socially with her peers—in their words, "to be like everyone else, and to be accepted by everyone." I understood their feelings. Through my studies (Turnbull and Turnbull 1986), I had come to realize that all parents have this goal for their children, no matter what their educational designations may be. We agreed that our decisions for Jamie throughout the year would be made with that goal foremost in our minds.

We also agreed that we would be very open with the other children and adults about Jamie's condition. This was consistent with my reading and with Laurie and Lambert's wishes. Children are naturally curious. The best way to help others accept and understand someone who is "different" is to answer their questions honestly and directly. Before long, we hoped, they would no longer see Jamie as "different."

Kindergarten

Finding our way

I want to make one thing very clear. This is not primarily a main-streaming story, and Jamie's physical condition and special-education status are not the main point. I've spent time discussing them because they help us know Jamie as an individual and understand the critical educational issues that affected her. But the fact remains that Jamie just happened to have a physical disability. Although this story takes a close look at an inclusive classroom, it is really about the incredible power of literacy and its role in enabling and enriching the life of one child, her family, and the larger community surrounding her.

. . . . .

Jamie started with us that September, all of us ready and eager to see how things would unfold. When we began the year, Jamie's reticence about talking to people she didn't know made things a bit awkward. I had to do a lot of talking for her. The other children asked many questions, as we had anticipated. I tried to answer them simply and directly: "Jamie can't walk because her leg muscles are not strong enough to hold her. She was born that way." "Her wheelchair helps her to move around, just like my glasses help me see better." "Jamie can't walk, but she can do many other things."

One thing I had learned from my reading was that children often fear they may "catch" a disability if they come into contact with a disabled person. We had many discussions and read numerous books to help class members learn more about various disabilities and to alleviate their worries about themselves. There are some wonderful stories dealing with this subject (e.g., *Someone Special, Just Like You* and *About Handicaps*), and I took advantage of everything I could find.

Although children ask a lot of questions, they readily accept honest answers. It didn't take long before the questions decreased and the other students were comfortable being with Jamie. And she began to smile at and talk a little with them.

It wasn't the same outside our classroom, though, because the rest of the students and staff were still strangers to Jamie. Some would stare or shy away. Some children—and even some adults—would move close to her and ask me, "What's her name?" I'd always answer, "Why don't you ask her?" We all harbor assumptions based on our experiences. At our school, up until this time, most of the students who were in wheelchairs had multiple handicaps and couldn't speak. Many people probably assumed that Jamie wasn't able to speak either. I enjoyed watching their surprise when Jamie told them her name! It reminded me again and again how much we lose when we let our preconceived notions get in our way.

In class, we trial-and-errored our way into a number of routines. The first changes were in the physical setup of the classroom. I wanted Jamie to be able to use as much of the room as possible, so we were constantly rearranging the furniture to provide navigable pathways. I hoped this would increase her feelings of independence.

The next change concerned the aide assigned to help Jamie. She was caring and competent and did her best to be helpful, but after a few weeks I realized that her constant presence in the classroom was a major barrier to Jamie's social progress. She hovered over Jamie all day, bringing her materials, cleaning up for her, talking with her, even selecting activities for her. One day, I watched a group of children invite Jamie to play house with them. At the same time, the aide brought Jamie a puzzle, spread it out on the table, and told Jamie to work on it with her. Jamie dutifully pushed the pieces around but looked longingly at the group playing house across the room. At that moment I fully understood that the aide, in her well-meaning way, was keeping Jamie separated from her classmates.

When Laurie picked Jamie up that afternoon, I mentioned my concerns. Our daily talks had helped Jamie's adjustment, and I wanted to hear the family's ideas. We were all there to help Jamie. Multiple perspectives and voices could only be beneficial.

We agreed we were now confident that the children were being gentle with Jamie. They were in fact quite protective of her, and our earlier fears that the chair would accidentally be tipped over were gone. We even no longer saw a need to "protect" Jamie at recess, because there were always children clustering around her.

We decided to have the aide come in only to take Jamie to the bathroom during recess and to help her during lunchtime. It was one of the best decisions we made; it was the beginning of real freedom for Jamie to be herself and to interact fully with others. We took a risk by not doing things the way they had been done before, but that's what we have to do when we make decisions. We have to think of the whole child and what might be best for that unique individual, then give it our best try. It's only then that we learn.

Full interaction can be hindered or enabled not just by human attitudes but also by the physical environment. If we're lucky, these physical aspects are relatively easy to correct. Inside our room, Jamie was now able to be with her classmates during all activities. Outside, she still had to stay on the walkways or on one small portion of the playground, because she couldn't maneuver her wheelchair safely down the steplike drop from the concrete to the larger grassy areas. Children would call to her to join them, and she'd watch them with the same longing I'd seen when she had to work the puzzle with her aide rather than play house with her friends. I spoke to my principal about this, and the next morning our custodians were out building little asphalt ramps just big enough for Jamie's wheelchair, giving her access to every area of the playground. It thrilled me—and amazed other adults—to see Jamie playing "chase" with her friends from then on.

Other, more touchy issues also surfaced as we went along and made me consider anew the meaning of "the whole child." One was going to the bathroom. Because Jamie's control of her lower-body muscles was inconsistent and because getting to a bathroom on time was not always feasible, she wore pull-up diapers. At recess, the aide was supposed to take Jamie to the health room (a reasonably private place) and lift her onto a potty chair. However, Jamie sometimes needed only to have her diaper changed, and the aide began doing so on a rug in a corner of our classroom instead of taking her to the health room. The aide was used to changing the diapers of the severely multiply handicapped students in their isolated classroom so her action was probably automatic, but I was upset. Jamie was small and needed to be carried, but she was not an infant, and she was very much aware of her surroundings. No one would have dreamed of putting her ambulatory classmates in such a situation! Jamie deserved to have her dignity preserved. I asked the aide to change Jamie only in the privacy of the health room, and the problem was solved.

These incidents may perhaps seem trivial, but the larger issues involved are fundamental. Sometimes we have to speak up for what we think is right for our students. If we don't advocate for them, perhaps no one will; we may be the only one aware of their situation. It's the sum total of these "small" things that make up the total quality of a child's educational experience. In fact, it's these small things that make quality education possible. Without them, Jamie would still have been "that girl in the wheelchair." Because of them, she became "Jamie"—to everyone.

Forming a community

At the beginning of the school year I wasn't sure how our curriculum would look, but I was committed to giving my students three main conditions for learning: large blocks of time in which to pursue reading and writing in depth; the opportunity to choose the particular activities they would pursue; and ownership of their learning. Since I was also convinced that learning is social, I made sure that small- and large-group interaction was a natural and continuous part of the process. Because I wanted the children to be able to help one another as much as possible, I tried to structure the classroom environment accordingly. I knew I needed to observe the children very closely in order to become aware of ways I might foster their collaboration.

In previous years, I had been the "all-knowing" teacher dispensing information and knowledge. The children came to me for everything, and I expected and accepted this. If a child asked me, How do you make a D? or, What can I write about? I would give the answer. There might be five or six other children waiting with questions; they'd just have to wait while I helped one at a time. I'd go home exhausted from answering questions all day.

When I changed my curriculum, I realized that if I wanted the children to collaborate, I would have to live and model that process myself. If someone asked me, How do you make a D? I'd say, Why don't you ask John? if I knew from my observations that John would be able to help. I also knew that by helping his classmate, John would become more aware of his own knowledge of language and his own literacy would grow.

It didn't take long for collaboration to establish itself as a natural part of our curriculum. I was happy; the children were working together and I was free to observe more and to spend more time with individuals. When children are given a chance to work together, they learn to know one another well, and they know exactly whom to seek out for the help they need. The beautiful part is that everyone can help someone in some way.

Jamie was already an accepted part of our class, and the other children were helping her with her physical needs. She would ask for help only with things she couldn't do, such as picking up her pencil if it dropped to the floor or getting a book she couldn't reach. I was glad that she had this desire to be as independent as possible and that the children were eager to help her whenever they could. But as I thought about my vision for learning in my classroom, I realized that something was missing. True collaboration means that everyone involved contributes. It wouldn't be enough for the children to help Jamie; she needed opportunities to help others.

I needn't have worried. Researchers in early literacy (Bissex 1980; Ferreiro and Teberosky 1982; Goodman 1986; Kamii et al. 1991) have taught us that children know a lot about literacy long before they enter school, "through their daily and mundane experiences in their particular social, cultural, religious, economic, linguistic, and literate societies" (Goodman 1986). Jamie's family had provided her many reading and writing experiences during her early years, and she came to school with the benefit of these experiences. Rich home literacy environments are not the exclusive province of college-educated professionals; they exist in all kinds of families and they can take many forms. Jamie's parents were high school graduates who considered books a priority in their home and transmitted this value to their children.

Jamie's classmates quickly found out without me that she could identify and write all the letters of the alphabet and that she had many ideas for writing, and they started asking her for help. She would always work with them patiently and happily. They also found out that she loved books and had a special fondness for humorous stories and illustrations. I would see children watching her as she turned the pages, smiling and chuckling to herself. I could sense their curiosity to find out what special secrets she so obviously knew. Soon they began inviting her to read with them. Their laughter as they enjoyed and discussed their favorite books together was an enticing invitation to others who didn't want to miss out on the fun. Little literature discussion groups started to spring up everywhere. This provided a natural context for Jamie's social development and validated my previous hunch that help needs to work two ways for true collaboration to take place.

Connecting with books

I love digging into educational research. I like knowing what other people have learned and connecting it to other things I've read and to my own life. But I don't read passively or accept statements at face value. When I find an idea that intrigues me, I want to try it out, make my own decisions about it and interpret it in my own way. That's one of the things that excites me about being a teacher.

I had been studying a lot about reader-response theory, which suggests that meaning is not inherent to the printed word but is only derived through the reader's construction of understanding (Cazden 1981; Rosenblatt 1978; Wells 1990). This construction can be enhanced when readers discuss books together, exploring meanings and sharing viewpoints. I had read that when students are given regular opportunities to respond to literature in this way, they will increase their oral competence and cognitive development, learn more about how stories work and explore them more deeply, and develop a more personal connection with books. Dewey had advocated this approach as far back as 1916!

It made sense to me. It sounded like real life. When I read a good or thought-provoking book, I can hardly contain myself. I'll rush to tell a family member or friend, "You have to read this book!" and then I can hardly wait until that person reads it so we can talk about it. Others do the same with me, and their enthusiasm makes me want to read the book they're recommending.

Invariably, as I talk with someone else about a book, I find new ways of thinking about it. There may be points that I have overlooked or that I have interpreted differently. We may take totally different views about a character, an event, or a theme and have a stimulating debate. In any case, I find myself thinking much more about the meaning of what I've read and returning to the text to consider it more deeply. I come away with a richer understanding and appreciation of the book.

Books have always been important in my life. I grew up in a literate family where books were valued. I was read to from the time I was very small. I believe that's why I became a reader. I've always wanted to provide my students with the same positive experiences with books, especially since many may not have such experiences in their own family. I like to make their school environment as homelike as possible, using good literature, lots of it, in my classroom. My studies convinced me that I wanted to extend their experiences even further.

Since I was looking for more authentic ways for my students to experience reading, I wanted to increase and improve their opportunities to respond to literature. Up till now, our book discussions had taken place informally or during whole-class story reading. Now I wanted more. As I observed the small-group book discussions that had begun so naturally with Jamie, I thought the next logical step would be to formalize these groups and conduct my own research study to determine their effectiveness. Most of the research I'd found concentrated on using literature discussion groups with older students. I was curious whether formalizing the discussions would make a difference for my young readers. I also wanted to learn more about how to carry out my role as observer and facilitator.

There wasn't a single "correct" model to follow, only certain broad guidelines that reflected a framework of belief and knowledge about literacy with which I identified. The purpose of the group should be to communicate and exchange meaning, not focus on isolated facts or answer someone else's questions. I needed to let the children choose what books to discuss. I needed to encourage them to respond to pictures as well as words, to return to the story as often as possible to amplify and clarify their ideas, and to share their interpretations and connections. I needed to value nonverbal as well as verbal responses and to encourage extensions to alternate modes of response such as drama, art, or music.

I needed to facilitate, not direct, the discussions, and to share my own responses openly, as both model and legitimizer. Most important of all, I had to listen to the children more and talk less, and be open to the new possibilities that might emerge. The few questions I asked had to be open-ended, designed to stimulate thought. It was a tall order, but I was ready to try.

I told the children that I could see how much we all enjoyed talking about the stories we read and that I was going to give them more time to do so, in what I called "literature study groups." I separated some books we had recently read and enjoyed into a pile and asked them to choose four that they would like to talk more about. We listed the four books on the chalkboard and each child signed his or her name under one of them. I explained that I would meet with one or two groups each day, while the rest of the class read or wrote independently, and we agreed that only emergency interruptions would be allowed during these meetings. Since it was now late fall and the children were working quite well independently, this structure seemed feasible.

Our literature study groups met throughout the rest of the year. The class looked forward to these meetings eagerly, just as I did. I was constantly delighted and amazed by the length and depth of the discussions. The children explored the illustrations in minute detail as they retold the stories to each other. They discussed their favorite parts over and over and freely expressed their feelings about characters and events.

Jamie, in her inimitable way, added humor and impetus to the talk and often helped the other children interpret the story. The following excerpt from a January discussion of *Henny Penny* shows this clearly:

ME: What do you think about Henny Penny?
JOHN: She was crazy.
PAT: She thought the sky was moving.
JAMIE: No, falling.

JOHN: She should have looked first.

PAT: But the fox tricked them.

JOHN: And the fox got wife and kids.

PAT: And they never saw the king.

DANIEL: And the king never knew the sky was falling.

JAMIE: She's a funny chicken, because she said the sky was falling.

ME: What do you think about the fox?

JAMIE: I'd whack the fox on the butt. (*Everyone laughs.*)

PAT: I'd cut off his tail.

JOHN: I'd choke him.

JACKIE: I'd get a rope, tie him up, and throw him in the rubbish can.
(*Everyone laughs.*)

JOHN: I didn't like it when he lied.

PAT: I was sad when he ate them.

Laughter was always a part of our discussions, and Jamie's sense of humor often triggered it. I think these joyful associations with literature were one reason the children hungered for more and more book talk. After a while, they suggested forming literature study groups for certain stories. I noticed that every book they selected for further discussion was one generally considered to be high-quality literature. The children were gaining an intuitive sense of what made a story worthy of their time and thought.

Sometimes their discussions led students to dramatize a story. One day in early March, five children, Jamie among them, decided to act out the story of *Swimmy*, one of their favorites, which we had already discussed in some depth. They asked me for colored tissue paper to make their costumes, and they set about planning the performance.

I usually allow the children to create their dramatic presentations on their own. I've found that the performance can be as short as thirty seconds and radically different from what they rehearsed, but it hardly matters. The value is in the process. They create, collaborate, debate, and decide, always returning to the details of the story to support their choices. It's fascinating to watch and involves rich and valuable learning.

The children began by deciding who would play which part. Bobby made a green costume and declared that he would be Swimmy. The others reminded him that Swimmy was black, so he asked me for black tissue paper, which I didn't have. I suggested he pretend it was black, but he said he'd just be green and pretend that Swimmy had gotten old. This satisfied everyone else.

Jamie was sitting on the rug with the other children, in her small wooden chair. She decided she would be the big tuna fish who chased after Swimmy and his family. As they planned their actions, the children kept looking in the book to check details. Several times Jamie kept the group focused on plot accuracy. For example, when Bobby directed the students playing Swimmy's family, "You guys run away," Jamie showed him the appropriate page in the book and reminded him, "In the story, only Swimmy ran away." Wanting to take the sting out of her contradiction, she added, "You gotta run away when we come. This is going to be fun!"

As the rehearsal progressed, Jamie gradually took on the roles of announcer, director, and performer. She invited the class to watch when the play was ready, made announcements at appropriate times, prompted the big fish when it was time for him to eat the smaller ones, and animatedly "swam" her part in her little chair. I couldn't believe that this confident leader was the same quiet girl I had met only a few short months ago! Literature was empowering her to reach far beyond herself.

The power of reader response lies in the way it helps us explore and personalize what we find in books. What I saw happening with Jamie and the other children gave me convincing evidence of this and motivated me to look for more response opportunities. I was thankful to Jamie for pointing the way for us to begin our explorations and for her active involvement and leadership.

Connecting with families

I was also beginning to explore reader-response possibilities as I searched for ways to improve our home-school connection. I had already instituted read-aloud "homework," commonly used in kindergartens, a few years earlier. I asked parents to read to their children every day and to record the titles read in logs that the children carried back and forth. I thought this would give the children the most important experience they would need to become successful readers, being read to by their parents.

But something kept nagging at me, and it grew more insistent each year. I had read and believed that "the single most important activity for building the knowledge required for eventual success in reading is reading aloud to children" (Anderson et al. 1985). But this statement carries the assumption that the read-aloud experience is a quality one, and I somehow felt that reading books just to list them in a log might not provide that quality. Besides, as a parent, I wasn't sure I would have appreciated the pressure of daily reading logs; I felt it might have taken away from the pleasure of shared reading.

As I studied the research on talking about books, I began to understand what I should have known all along had I thought more about my own childhood experiences with books: it isn't only the reading but the responses and interactions that go with it that provide the context for true literacy development.

I realized that reader response and social interaction were the missing elements in my home read-aloud program. Some families might be aware of these elements or incorporate them intuitively, but others might not. In any case, I thought it could be useful to make these elements more explicit and give them the value they deserved.

Reader-response journals are widely used in classrooms, but those I had read about seemed to be used mostly with children old enough to write their own entries. Yet children of any age respond to reading, and I wanted it to be an integral part of my kindergarteners' reading experiences, not just at school but at home. I decided to try a reader-response journal that parents and children could keep together. I hoped this would make the home read-aloud times more meaningful and enjoyable. I also hoped it would complement the response approach I was trying to encourage in my classroom.

In November, I invited parents and children to an evening workshop, during which I briefly explained the rationale for a reader-response approach to literature, read a story aloud to them, and modeled response-type discussion and questions as opposed to those seeking mere recall of information.

I then described what I was asking the parents to do: continue reading and discussing stories with their children as much as possible, but twice a week (to keep it pleasurable and to avoid the pressure that comes with having to do something every day) extend that reading to a journal entry. I asked the parents to write a few things the child said about the story during the discussion and then the child could draw a picture about the story and dictate or write something about the picture. I would read and respond to the journals as they were turned in.

We held a short practice session, with each parent-child grouping trying out the reading and journal recording. Informal discussion and questions followed, and after some light refreshments, each family went home with their journal (a hard-covered composition tablet) and a new storybook. The whole process took only about an hour, and everyone seemed enthusiastic.

The journals became an important part of school life for at least two-thirds of our families. I sent evaluation surveys home periodically, and parents responded that they found the journals fun and useful for developing both family closeness and their children's literacy. The students also seemed very positive about the journals and often reminded their parents to make time for them. I still worried about reaching the families who weren't participating, but I was feeling good about those who were.

Jamie's family took to the journal like the proverbial duck to water. Her parents had read to Jamie from her earliest years, and it seemed a natural step to begin writing about the books they enjoyed together. Although everyone in Jamie's family eventually took part in the reading, Laurie made most of the journal entries. This was her first entry, for *Moon Mouse:*

Jamie's favorite part of the book is when Arthur's mom said, "Lucky thing you didn't eat the whole moon up!"

And the book is funny 'cause Arthur thinks the moon is made of cheese. What a silly mouse!

Laurie and Lambert read the story to Jamie together. Jamie made some small drawings of the building with the steps that Arthur climbed to look for the moon, and Lambert helped draw Arthur. Laurie told me how much fun they all had sharing the story and writing about it. I was pleased.

Their next entry, for a story about a boy and his new bike, was made two days later. Jamie's brother Jarrett read the book to her and she wrote the following sentence, all in capitals: "MY GRANDMA'S FRIEND BOUGHT A NEW BIKE FOR MY BROTHER." Laurie continued:

Jamie insisted she write the above. She said when she first read the book (she won it in Mrs. Parker's class), she immediately thought of Jarrett getting his new bike.

She said her cousins Cory Ann and Natalie would like the picture on page 9 (she marked the page numbers herself) because that's how her brother looked, too. He was too big for the bike! His knees were sticking out!

Moon Mouse
  by Adelaide Holl

11-07-90
Read by: Daddy &
            Mommy

   Jamie's favorite part of the book is when Arthur's mom said, "Lucky thing you didn't eat the whole moon up!"
   And the book is funny cause Arthur thinks the moon is made of cheese. What a _silly_ mouse!

Daddy helped draw Arthur

building w/ steps

You're right – he is _very_ silly! I'm glad you like this book – I _do_, too!

Thank you for coming to our meeting! ☺

26

Mike's New Bike
  by Rose Greydanus

11-09-90

Read by: Jarrett
  Panui (brother)

MY GRANDMA'S
FRIEND BOUGHT
A NEW BIKE FOR
MY BROTHER.

↑ Jamie _insisted_ she write the above. She said
when she first read the book, (she won it in
Mrs Parker's class) she immediately thought of
Jarrett getting his new bike.

  She said her cousins CoryAnn : Natalie
would like the picture on page 9, (she marked
the page numbers herself) because that's how her
brother looked like too. He was _too big_ for the
bike!   His knees were sticking out!

            I remember being too big
            for my bike, too. It makes a
            funny picture!
              Good thinking, Jamie – and
            good writing, too!

27

I was excited; two significant things were happening. First, Jarrett was becoming involved with the reading. Second, Jamie was already making personal connections with books. I hoped this would continue and was curious to see what other interesting things would emerge.

I didn't have to wait long to find out. The next week, I read Laurie's entry for *My Dog and the Knock Knock Mystery*:

This was Jamie's first mystery book. I explained what "mystery" meant, but I think she still doesn't quite fully understand. This word is still a "mystery" to her. Ha! Ha!

Towards the ending of the story, I asked her to try and solve the mystery herself. She guessed that the apples were the answer to the mystery. She was correct! She said the pictures gave her the answer.

I was growing more excited. I could see evidence here of so many things that Laurie was encouraging naturally and that, according to research, were important for children to experience in order to become readers. Laurie was helping Jamie develop her vocabulary, predict what might happen next, and use pictures to help her understand the story. I also realized where Jamie got her sense of humor!

Laurie continued to keep the journal faithfully with Jamie. They discussed favorite characters and their motivations, favorite incidents, new words encountered, and real and make-believe aspects of the stories, and they continued to share their personal connections with the stories. I was starting to feel as if I knew all the family well, even relatives whom I hadn't met, because so many were mentioned in the journal.

Soon Jamie's Grandma Lo began to participate. One day she read *One Fish, Two Fish, Red Fish, Blue Fish* to Jamie. Laurie wrote:

Jamie just remembers that this book is so very silly! What she loved so dearly was Grandma's uncontrollable laughter! It was a delight and a surprise for me as well. I can't remember the last time I saw my mom actually read a book! Watching my mom read to my little girl was very special!

I was touched by Laurie's feelings. Through their shared reading, family members were making new discoveries and forming new relationships with one another. One book, about a new baby in a household, led to a conversation about Jamie's arrival in her own family:

We talked about Jarrett wanting a sister very badly and how happy he was when Jamie was born. Jamie was thrilled to find out that Jarrett was the person who thought of her name.

I noticed as the year went on that Jamie was sharing in more of the reading. The journal page headings indicated that stories were read by "Mom and Jamie," "Dad and Jamie," "Jarrett and Jamie," or "Grandma and Jamie." I also noticed that their conversations about the books had changed. Earlier, they had focused mostly on retelling the plot and responding briefly to the story. Now they were branching out to more diverse life and literature connections, as books reminded them of other books and family experiences.

Jamie was also expressing her opinions about various stories more freely; if she disliked a book, she said so. I was glad to see her becoming more discriminating in her taste and learning more about her preferences. I thought this was an important real-life issue, so we discussed it as a whole class one day. We agreed that we can't possibly like every book we read and that this is okay, especially since there are so many wonderful books waiting to be read. We also talked about why we do like certain books. I hoped this would start the children thinking more about the common characteristics of good literature.

By May, Jamie was able to read several books all by herself. I remember how thrilled I was the first time Jamie's name was listed at the top of the journal page as the sole reader. I could visualize the scene and their excitement as I read Laurie's entry for *Over in the Meadow*:

Jamie read this nursery counting rhyme book aloud to her daddy! Lambert said Jamie really enjoyed the rhyming words and the familiar tune! She was very proud that the counting came so easy for her. . . . She knew a lot of the words, and for others, she looked at the pictures first, then knew the words, such as lizards, beavers, etc. She made the association!

Jamie's dad said he feels so <u>proud</u> and <u>happy</u> to have Jamie Girl <u>read to him</u> for a change! He relaxed in bed while Jamie <u>anxiously</u> and very <u>proudly</u> read OUT LOUD (of course!) and very clearly! She's grown up!

A few days later, Laurie revealed her own feelings about Jamie's emergence as a reader:

Jamie read this book, <u>Green Eggs and Ham</u>, all by herself! The cover of the book says, "I Can Read It All By Myself" and it's true! My husband and I are so excited and happy about this achievement. Jamie has always told us that she was anxious to read—and she's arrived! Thank you so much, Mrs. Parker! I truly believe these journals are a wonderful thing!

I read this entry with tears in my eyes. I felt so privileged to share this special milestone with Jamie's family! It was just like being there when my own children took their first step, said their first word, or began to read. It made the journal experiment, and the year, worthwhile.

When children begin to read, it seems to just "happen"; even with all we've learned about reading, how it actually comes about is still a mystery—a miracle, really, when we consider all it involves. I didn't know exactly what made it happen for Jamie, but I felt more strongly than ever that immersion in good literature and a strong home-school partnership were key factors in unlocking the process for her. Laurie seemed to agree. When I asked the parents to evaluate their feelings about various aspects of the journal experience, she wrote:

We have such a variety of books, the vocabulary naturally increases. It forms a relationship between the person reading the book and Jamie. It makes the adult learn to ask proper or appropriate questions concerning the book. We are forced to listen, as we must put down Jamie's views/comments on paper. Results can be very uplifting, surprising, and

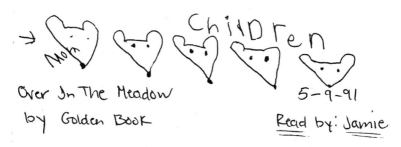

Mom   ChilDren

Over In The Meadow   5-9-91
by Golden Book

<u>Read by</u>: <u>Jamie</u>

Jamie read this nursery counting rhyme book aloud to her daddy! 😊 Lambert said Jamie really enjoyed the rhyming words and the familiar tune! She was very proud that the counting came so easy for her. She said she not only could recognize the number words such as five, six, etc., but she could also tell by the pictures. They showed five bees, six birds, etc. She knew a lot of the words, and for others, she looked at the pictures first, then knew the words, such as lizards, beavers, etc. She made the association!

Jamie's dad said he feels so <u>proud</u> and <u>happy</u> to have Jamie girl <u>read</u> <u>to</u> ~~him~~ for a change! He relaxed in bed while Jamie <u>anxiously</u> and very <u>proudly</u> read OUT LOUD (of course!) and very clearly! She's grown up! →<u>Yes!!</u>

· <u>Terrific!</u> 😊

31

funny; many times, we realize Jamie's thoughts and expressions are wonderful! Always very interesting! I personally have found it more meaningful and enjoyable to really discuss books in detail than to list many books just for the sake of reading them. . . . The journal gives the chance to really take the time and discover Jamie's feelings, opinions. . . . The best thing is finding out what Jamie feels, discusses, the many surprises!

As I reflected on Laurie's words and on the school year, I marveled at the many surprises I had experienced with all my students and on how things had changed for Jamie in particular. Socially, she had progressed far beyond Laurie and Lambert's expectations. She was not just an accepted member of the class, she had become an acknowledged leader and a magnet to whom others were drawn. She zoomed into the classroom every morning in her "hot rod" wheelchair, bright-eyed, smiling, and eager to plunge into the day's activities. Her social interests and desires were those of her friends—dolls, jewelry, clothes, games, birthday parties, even boys!

Academically, there was no doubt that Jamie had progressed. Her developing literacy was apparent. Reading and writing were meaningful and joyful parts of her life, and through her enthusiasm she had drawn others into literacy as well. I couldn't have asked for more. I fully believed that without the social interactions and choices made possible by our curricular structure, she would not have had the opportunities to grow as she did.

My one regret was that I would now have to send my students on to another teacher. Our little classroom community had formed a close bond over the year. The children's growth had been exciting. I was thankful for our time together, and I didn't want it to end. I wished we could continue so I could see what might happen next, especially with Jamie.

First Grade

Strengthening the bonds

Timing is everything. For the first time in many years, there was a first-grade position available for the following school year. I decided I couldn't pass up the opportunity. Since lower-grade students at our school are randomly assigned to heterogeneous classes each year, I wouldn't be able to keep all my kindergarten students, but I knew I would have at least a few of them. I saw it as a good chance to learn for myself where all this reading and writing excitement might lead.

I ended up with four students who had been with me in kindergarten, including Jamie. I was happy I'd be working with her for another year. It made sense, too. Since our relationships and working routines were already established, we wouldn't have to waste valuable time adjusting all over again.

Jamie's family had supported her reading and writing throughout the summer, providing her with a wide variety of books and time to share and enjoy them together. Knowing how much she loved to write, they also kept her supplied with paper and notepads, which she filled with labeled drawings, short notes, and a variety of lists. Many of the materials encouraged and enabled her to incorporate writing naturally as she played with Jarrett. As Laurie said, "They were always writing." With a set of blank sales receipt forms and Grandma Lo's old checkbook, they spent hours playing store, restaurant, and bank. They loved giving each other receipts for "one private plane, $1,200," or "one mansion, $9,400," as they explored various uses of writing in the world of business.

Writing was just as natural and important when they played house. On one occasion, Jamie (the "mother") wrote instructions for Jarrett (the "father"), who was supposed to be taking care of the "baby":

Chores for Baby
1. Change diaper.
2. Feed.
3. Play with it.
4. Make it take a nap.
5. Teach the baby.
6. Read and sing songs.

It was easy to see from this list how much she valued reading.

By September 1991 Jamie was a fluent and avid reader who loved to read, write, and talk. Even though only three of her former classmates were with her in the new class, everyone else already knew her from all the socializing that had gone on outside the classroom. Jamie again assumed her leadership role quite naturally, helping others with reading and writing and drawing them into literacy through her own enjoyment of books.

She continued to form close friendships with many of her classmates. I noticed, though, that these social relationships were evolving. Before, they had focused mostly on dolls and parties; now, they seemed to focus more on book talk, often initiated by Jamie. Our literacy club was thriving, again thanks to Jamie's enthusiasm.

One of the children's favorite times each day was when I read to them from our ongoing chapter books. Because these books usually have few pictures, we had talked about the need for the children to "make their own pictures in their minds"; so they devised a daily ritual of turning off the lights and lying down with their eyes closed to help them do this. They looked forward to this time so much that they reminded me if they thought I had forgotten.

As adults, we encounter books we cannot bear to put down; we just have to read on, no matter what other work might be waiting. So it was with my first graders. When they became totally involved in a good story, they would beg for "just one more chapter." Sometimes I'd indulge them; other times, knowing the value of their being left wanting more, I'd put the book away on my desk and we'd go on to other things.

It was Jamie who instigated the "book raids." On days when she and her friends felt they couldn't possibly wait another moment to find out what happened next in the story, they would (at Jamie's whispered suggestion) "sneak" the book from my desk at the first opportunity (as I pretended not to notice) and drive themselves relentlessly to read on, helping each other struggle through the text and giggling at their cleverness in fooling me. I was amazed at how much they were able to read on their own, and I learned a valuable lesson by observing for myself what is possible when students pursue their own inquiries. So often children's learning is hindered by the limits placed on them by traditional school curriculums. Although these chapter books were not meant to be read independently by typical first graders, Jamie and her friends didn't know that and weren't bound by arbitrary, artificial "reading levels."

Jamie's coconspirators in the book raids were also her closest friends: Cari, Annie, Mayra, and Jamilee. As they shared more and more at school, they naturally wanted to be together after school as well. At first, they did this by phone. They delighted in looking up one another's numbers in the telephone directory we kept in our classroom, and each girl created her own personal directory. Laurie told me they talked on the phone nearly every day. This was especially helpful on the days when Jamie was not well enough to go to school, for it linked her to her classmates when she could not be with them in person.

After a while, the girls began playing at one another's homes after school and on weekends. But even when Jamie was well enough for social visits, there were many constraints. Laurie always had to accompany her to friends' houses to tend to her physical needs. And Jamie could never spend the night at her friends' houses. But she could and did have friends visit often, even sleep over, although usually just one at a time, to decrease her risk of exposure to germs and infection. Mostly, Jamie accepted these limitations without complaint, but there were days when her disappointment surfaced and she would grumble angrily,

"Why can't I go?" or "How come I have to miss the party?" She would tell her parents that they were "the meanest people in the world" and that she was going to "run away from home," whereupon she would maneuver her wheelchair as fast and as far as she could (which wasn't very fast or very far) until she had calmed down. I understood. Jamie wasn't able to relieve her frustration through vigorous physical activity, and she also knew her situation wasn't temporary. It must have been unbearable at times.

Fortunately, our school routines were less complex, and providing for Jamie's physical needs in the classroom no longer seemed anything out of the ordinary. It was as natural a part of our lives as she was. When we built a life-sized playhouse out of cardboard cartons, it was the children who said, "We have to make sure we build the door wide enough for Jamie's wheelchair to fit." When they mixed the cookie dough for our housewarming party, they helped her stir, knowing she was not strong enough to do it herself. When we went to assemblies or the library, the children remembered to take along her small wooden chair; in fact, they vied for the chance to carry it.

On field trips, which we had at least once a month, Laurie would bring along a collapsible stroller, since it allowed Jamie easier access to some areas. The children always helped carry the stroller and any other equipment Laurie might bring.

One of our students, Kenneth, was extremely shy and unsure of himself. He was a thoughtful and sensitive child, the kind who can easily be overlooked by a teacher or intimidated by a group of active, noisy youngsters. I worried about him a lot, because he seemed to lack the confidence to take either social or academic risks.

Kenneth, in turn, often worried about Jamie. He would tell me softly that he was afraid her legs might never get stronger. He told me he used to dream about her, and in his dreams she was able to walk. He was always very solicitous of her, quietly volunteering to help her in any way he could.

Kenneth watched various children carry and set up Jamie's stroller on our outings. After a while, he began approaching Laurie and offering his services before we even started out. I guess he wanted to make sure no one would beat him to it. I don't think Kenneth would ever have asserted himself publicly, yet his desire to help Jamie was so strong that in his quiet way, he somehow let it be known that he had taken over this duty. Kenneth became our "official" stroller person, and no one challenged his self-appointed status for the remainder of the year.

That responsibility did wonders for Kenneth's confidence. Laurie helped a lot, too, by always letting him know how much she appreciated his help. I think it was his growing feeling of self-worth that paved the way for Kenneth's growth in other areas. He began to smile often, to speak up in class, and to show academic progress.

Early in the year, Kenneth's writing usually consisted of one sentence at most, and that sentence would be made up of "safe" words, those he could spell without help. "I like school" was typical of what he would produce during an hour or more of writing time. As Kenneth became more confident in his role of stroller helper, he started writing about Jamie. At first, he filled several pages with details of his dreams about her. Later, he began to write about other things that were important to him.

Laurie and I spoke often about the way Kenneth was blossoming. The more he helped Jamie, the more, it seemed, he helped himself. Teachers hear a lot nowadays about the importance of developing our students' self-esteem. Whenever I think about Kenneth, I am reminded that true self-esteem lies not in empty words of flattery or "star student" bumper stickers but in the satisfaction of knowing that we have made a genuine contribution.

Laurie was developing a strong relationship with the other students as well as with Kenneth, since she spent so much time with us on our trips. Being a very outgoing person, she got to know each child well. She also began helping us periodically in the classroom, reading to and with the children and sharing some of her family's special books. These books provided a connection between the class and the rest of Jamie's family.

When we were studying about space, Laurie mentioned to me that Jarrett was very interested in that topic and had a good collection of related books. He willingly loaned us some of them, including a giant-sized book about the planets. The children loved that book so much they almost memorized it, and they were hungry for more information. I had heard about a special open house for elementary school students that was being held by the University of Hawai'i Planetary Sciences Department, so we went. We invited Jarrett to go with us, and we arranged for him to meet and talk with one of the planetary science professors during the visit. Jarrett was thrilled with the new information he obtained, and my students were thrilled with their new big brother!

Lambert was seldom able to visit our class because of his work schedule, but he was a presence there nevertheless. The children loved acting out their favorite stories through dramatizations and puppet shows. We turned the tables on their sides or used cardboard boxes as puppet stages, which worked fine. Yet I always wished for a sturdy, permanent puppet center for my room, even though I knew one was way beyond my budget or that of the school. But what wonderful resources parents can be! Lambert donated a beautiful puppet center, which he made from scrap materials during his spare time. That one piece of classroom equipment created a multitude of possibilities for the children's creative expression, not just for puppets but for all sorts of dramatic play and opportunities to mirror real life. As the children wrote their thank-you letters to Lambert, their connection with Jamie's family was complete.

I always encourage letter writing in my classroom; I think it provides a real, worthwhile purpose for writing. We write group and individual letters for every appropriate social occasion, and I invite the children to write informally to anyone at any time. During her first-grade year, Jamie began to use letters in personally meaningful ways.

When Theodore Geisel (Dr. Seuss) passed away in September, we spent about two weeks celebrating his life. We read about him and we gathered as many of his books as we could, sharing them over and over. The children expressed their sadness that he would not be able to write any more books and their gratitude that what he did write would always be here with us.

Toward the end of that period, Jamie told me, "I think I'm going to write a letter to Dr. Seuss today." I was bewildered. Didn't she understand that he was dead? I didn't know what was going through her mind, but I didn't want to discourage her either. I just asked whether she would share her letter with me when she was finished. She agreed. Her letter, transcribed below, was a lesson for me that we should never assume what children understand or don't understand. We need to find out from them what they are really thinking.

> *10-4-91*
> *From Jamie*
> *to Dr. Seuss*
> *We like your*
> *books and*
> *the school*
> *likes your books.*
> *We hope you will*
> *feel better*
> *in heaven.*

Jamie's interest in all kinds of writing was growing, but she couldn't write as much as she wanted to because her arm muscles were so weak. It required a great deal of effort to exert enough pressure on her pencil to make her writing readable. That was fine when she was just beginning and writing short pieces, but now she had much more to say and she became fatigued long before she had said it all.

Again, Laurie and I talked about possible adjustments we could make. Laurie had noticed at home that Jamie enjoyed using her markers or other pens. She thought perhaps this was not just because of their bright colors—maybe they were easier to write with. It hadn't occurred to me that using a pencil might be creating a problem for Jamie, but now I thought, Why do we all have to do things the same way? We told Jamie it was okay for her to use pens or markers exclusively at school unless she preferred to use a pencil for a particular task. It was another good collaborative decision, a small but crucial adaptation that enabled her writing to flow.

Shaping our values

Laurie's writing was flowing, too, in the reader-response journal I was again requesting of the parents. I was amazed and delighted by her entries, and I learned from them constantly. I saw in them undeniable evidence of the growth that occurs with well-supported immersion in literature.

There was no doubt that Jamie's vocabulary was increasing. Again, Laurie seemed to encourage this naturally within the context of each story. On October 10, 1991, they read a book called *Copycat*. At the top of the journal page, Laurie listed the words she helped Jamie with as they read the story together: *bold, lurks, shed, sprawls, pigsty, grunts, sow, drakes, heather, kennel, croak, flits, fro, dusk, scuttles, squeaks, clucks, pecks, fowls, startles, outscreeching, trots, stable, neighs, mare, hillside.* (She continued listing new vocabulary all year. It helped me appreciate the increasing complexity of the books Jamie was reading.) In the text of her entry, Laurie commented: "There were a lot of new words I introduced to Jamie. She noticed some of these words were sounds animals make, i.e. 'croak' and 'neighs.' 'Flits to and fro' for the bats were both new to us." It must have been a good lesson for Jamie to find out that adults can learn new words, too!

This shared learning happened many times. When they read *A Cache of Jewels,* a book about collective nouns, Laurie wrote:

Jamie said she believes the word "cache" in this book title means "a bunch" or "plenty." She was looking at the pictures and we were discussing nouns and what it meant. She recalled a <u>bunch</u> of bananas, a <u>gam</u> of whales, a <u>school</u> of fish, a <u>forest</u> of trees, and an <u>army</u> of ants more easily than the others . . .

[I] knew of "nouns," but haven't heard of "collective" nouns for a while. Learning, or should I say relearning, some things is refreshing!

I was impressed with the variety of ways Laurie helped Jamie try to figure out word meanings. Sometimes Laurie was surprised, too. In one story, they encountered the word *vanish*. Laurie wrote: "Jamie said 'vanish' means gone. Her mom thought she knew this because of the pictures. Jamie said it was because her dad told her what it meant. Ha, ha!"

I was also impressed with the way Laurie intuitively helped Jamie reinforce her newly acquired vocabulary: "For the word 'boost,' Jamie asked me what it meant. So I gave her a boost, and she said it meant 'to lift up.' We thought it was fun to do that! Now she always asks me to give her a 'boost'!!"

As the year went on, I saw subtle changes in their talk about words, as they began discussing multiple meanings and different shades of meaning. In one discussion, Laurie reported: "Jamie knew the word 'grand' meant nice and beautiful, but we also shared it to be huge, big." (This was the meaning as they interpreted it from the story.) As part of this same entry, Laurie had written that Jamie "chuckled" at a particular name, adding this note: "I put 'chuckled' on purpose, and Jamie scolded me and told me to put something simple like 'laughed.'" Honoring Jamie's ownership of the journal, Laurie replaced *chuckled* with *laughed*.

By spring, I could easily see the difference in the new vocabulary words Jamie and Laurie were discussing. This was the list from *Solomon the Rusty Nail*, on May 17, 1992: *pazoozle, chomped, chard, Parcheesi, discombobulated, brainsick, savory, doily, goggle-eyed, hasenpfeffer, indelibly, tactless, embedded, incinerated, somersault, carnivore*. It was a list worthy of any college entrance examination, yet Jamie was learning these words with ease and enjoyment.

A Cache of Jewels
 and Other Collective Nouns
By Ruth Heller

10-14-91

Read : Mom

Jamie said she believes the word 'cache' in this book title means 'a bunch' or 'plenty'. She was looking at the pictures and we were discussing nouns and what it meant. She recalled a <u>bunch</u> of bananas, a <u>gam</u> of whales, a <u>school</u> of fish, a <u>forest</u> of trees, and an <u>army</u> of ants more easily than the others.

She didn't like the <u>coven</u> of witches picture. It was spooky to her.

This was a delightful book with nice, big pictures. I think the reader enjoyed it more. The reader knew of 'nouns', but haven't heard of 'collective' nouns for awhile. Learning or shoul

True! I say re-learning some things are refreshing!

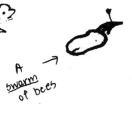

A
<u>bouquet</u>
of Flowers

A
<u>swarm</u>
of bees

Jamie, when we talk about nouns in our class, you can be my helper!

Laurie also recognized and helped facilitate Jamie's growing awareness of other language and writing conventions:

Jamie said this book was very easy to read. She knew all the words. She also read with the expressions, such as ! with excitement, ? questioned, and I got excited when she put the emphasis on the capitalized word: "This IS fun!"

She recognized all the contractions in the book!—I'd, aren't, hadn't, didn't, I'll, they're, I'm, wasn't, can't.

Jamie said the following are compound words: moonbeam, moonlight, fairyland, cannot, and haystack.

I felt this validated the approach I was using in my classroom. Some people mistakenly assume that a nontraditional approach to reading instruction ignores such skills, but that isn't so. The difference is that they are taught in the context of reading and enjoying whole stories, rather than as isolated, meaningless drill and practice. Proficient readers must be able to make use of meaning, syntax, and phonics in a balanced, flexible way. No responsible teacher neglects any of these elements, and others who accuse them of doing so need to stop sitting in judgment and educate themselves further in order to dispel the myths they perpetuate so unthinkingly.

Jamie and Laurie regularly analyzed and compared stories with increasing sophistication throughout the year. I was struck by the difference between these entries and the early kindergarten ones, which had dealt more with surface plot features. When they read a Hawaiian version of *The Three Little Pigs*, Laurie wrote:

Jamie told me the differences between this Hawaiian version and the original Three Little Pigs version. First of all, the pua'a keiki (Jamie guessed it to mean "little children"; it means "pig children") had parents. Jamie said the original version doesn't say they had parents. Second, this has a mean shark and the other has a mean wolf. And of course, the pili grass, the driftwood, and the lava rock are different from the straw, the sticks, and the bricks. Also, this new version has some Hawaiian words. Jamie said she didn't know "pau" was a Hawaiian word. Overall, Jamie prefers the original version simply because she said she hears about it more often than the new Hawaiian version.

One of the most important things Laurie did throughout the year was to continue to read to or with Jamie, even when the books were ones Jamie could have read by herself: "Although this was a simple, easy-to-read story, Jamie wanted her mom to read this story aloud to her. She also enjoyed the pictures." Sometimes I hear parents say, I can't wait for my children to read on their own so I don't have to read to them anymore. When I can, I do my utmost to convince them not to stop reading to their children, ever. We are never too old to enjoy being read to. My husband and I still read to each other! I think we form bonds with literature because of the human bonds we form as we share it. Jamie knew the comfort books can provide, and it helped her through some trying times:

Jamie said her brother, Jarrett, read her a book one night and helped make her fall asleep. That night, her parents went to a wedding party. She missed them, so her brother comforted her by reading to her.

Jamie had to miss out on her class field trip today because of illness. We spent the day reading lots of her favorites and talked about the rainy day. She felt better!

Jarrett read to Jamie often, and he seemed to enjoy their talks as much as she did: "Jarrett talked to her about the Plains Indians. . . . He did a project on the Plains Indians at school and it was enjoyable to see the kids share about what they read."

Perhaps because Jamie's family read to her so much, she began wanting to do the same for others. When she found a book she especially enjoyed, she couldn't wait to share it: "She also said she's going to read aloud to her cousin Christine this very same story."

I was certainly happy to see the development of Jamie's reading skills. But much more significant to me was the development I saw in personal and family values and relationships as Jamie and her family discussed books and shared their feelings in more and more depth. Laurie captured the richness of these discussions in detail:

Jamie was surprised to find out that while she was working on this journal, her dad was watching a baseball game on TV. Her dad started to explain to the kids what the World Series was, etc. And we all found out that Dad's dream is to someday watch a World Series game in person! [From a discussion of a book about baseball]

Jamie knows that [certain relatives and family friends] *are divorced. . . . When Jamie was asked about how she would feel if her parents got divorced, she said, "You almost did, remember?" We talked about a situation and I had to explain that couples argue from time to time but that doesn't mean they want to get divorced. She was almost three years old at that time and she recalled an argument her parents had. Interesting!* [From a discussion of a book about divorce]

Jamie said people should love people for their kindness and not their looks. And people should not break promises.

Jamie believes this story is about our world that is dying. She mentioned that she is helping save the world by picking up rubbish and other stuff.

I could see in these and similar examples proof of the humanizing power of literature. What a wonderful vehicle for sharing our values with our children! What a wonderful way for our children to explore their own values!

As I had done the year before, I asked parents for periodic evaluations of the journal process. In February, Laurie wrote:

Jamie's love for reading has really grown. She reads every day. . . . The choices of books are plentiful, enjoyable, and informative (and sometimes very personal and touching). Jamie likes it best when she reads with ease. She seems so confident and acts like such a "big girl" when reading aloud. She snuggles up to us and really loves it when it's our turn to read to her.

Through these journals, I have come to realize how much Jamie really can comprehend. She can read through a book once, close it, and recall either the main theme or the characters. She makes a lot of sense, and has good ideas and thoughts.

I get embarrassed sometimes when I'm scolded by Jamie for rewording her thoughts. She'll tell me what to write in the journal, and I'll write the words that I think would sound better. She'll check it over and correct me. I get so involved in the journals, I sometimes forget it's Jamie's journal. I have to word it her way.

I'll never forget how excited and proud I felt when Jamie read her first book all by herself! Now that she knows how to read, it's reading different types of books with lots of new words introduced to her. We also discover her favorite authors and illustrations, and her reasoning.

She really got off on a great start with these journals. It'll probably leave a lasting impression throughout her lifetime, and ours, too!

At the end of the school year, Laurie again shared her thoughts:

Well, another year of "Reading Journals" has come and gone. Thank you for introducing this during Jamie's kindergarten year. Lambert and I will never forget the joy we experienced when our little girl read all by herself! Of course, we have her journal for keepsakes. Our family really got closer and realized how enjoyable reading is and can be through this type of journal. Having to do these disciplined my family in taking the time out, first of all, and then enjoying the children's input, thoughts, experiences, drawings, etc., when discussing the story.

My goal will be to try and keep the kids' love for reading enjoyable and take the time to enjoy everyone's input. I'll also remember to keep Jamie's first diary "private" and try not to peek. Ha!

Once again, I felt sadness that the school year would soon come to a close. I had experienced for myself the joy and power of keeping my students for more than one year, and again I wished it didn't have to end. There was so much more I wanted and needed to learn.

Second Grade

Becoming a family

Sometimes wishes do come true. Shortly before the end of the school year, my principal called me in for a conference: The projected class enrollments for next year were unevenly distributed in the lower grades, and he had to assign a teacher to a combination first and second grade. He was doing this reluctantly, because he knew many teachers didn't like combination classes. But I had once mentioned that I'd like to try such an arrangement. Was I still interested and would I take the class?

My thoughts raced. I realized the learning opportunity, the incredibly exciting challenge I was being offered, and I wanted to jump at the chance. But I also realized I'd better make sure he understood what I hoped to do. I told him I'd love to try it, as long as he would give me the freedom to work with the students as an ungraded group and to construct my own curriculum with them, and as long as I could keep half of my present class as my second graders. He agreed at once. I will always be thankful to him for trusting me as a learner in the same way I try to trust my students.

I was to have ten first graders and ten second graders. I selected my second graders carefully, making sure I kept children who represented a wide range of academic, social, and emotional development. This had to be a true heterogeneous group, just like any other class at our school. I needed this diversity if things were to work as I hoped.

Our administrators traditionally made class assignments; parental choice was ordinarily not part of the process. I felt, though, that this situation was different. This type of class was new for our school. Some parents might have reservations about an ungraded, rather unorthodox curricular structure. Or they might be uneasy about having their children with me for the second or third year in a row. I felt a strong need for parental support in order to work effectively with the children. I asked and received my principal's permission to tell parents that their children were being assigned to my class, so that they could discuss it as a family and make sure they were comfortable with it.

Nine of the ten families agreed wholeheartedly. The parents of the tenth child explained that their hesitation was not based on any personal criticism—they had been satisfied with their child's education so far. But he had been in my class for two years, since kindergarten, and to them three years in a row with the same teacher was unheard of. They also worried that the first graders might "hold him back." I had had an excellent working relationship with this family for the past two years. I felt that if I forced the situation, it could undermine this relationship and could certainly affect their child in the long run. I asked my principal to place this boy in a different classroom; instead I took a student who had not been in my first grade class but who had been with me in kindergarten. I was never sorry I made this decision; it worked out well for everyone. The bottom line in true home-school collaboration has to be the child's welfare. It should never be a matter of ego or power. We're all on the same side; we want the best for our children.

Of course, I wanted to keep Jamie, partly for selfish reasons: I was fascinated with her literacy growth and I enjoyed and benefited from her presence in my classroom. Then, too, I recalled her easy transition from kindergarten to first grade and felt that another easy transition would make the most sense for her. Again, time wouldn't be wasted working out physical arrangements and routines in a new classroom. I was happy and grateful when Laurie and Lambert enthusiastically approved.

I spent a good part of the summer reading about multiage grouping and thinking about organizational and curricular possibilities. I knew generally what I wanted and didn't want. I envisioned this combination class not as separate grade levels but as one community of teachers and learners, all of us, including me, playing both roles as we lived and worked together. In keeping with this goal, I decided to call our group the Primary 'Ohana (Hawaiian for *family*) class.

I wanted my curriculum to deal with broad themes and concepts rather than a narrow hierarchy of skills. Such a curriculum would be consistent with my emerging view of literacy development and with my move, based on my continued studies, toward an increasingly holistic approach to learning. It would, I felt sure, enable me to deal with the wide age and developmental range of my students. Since I intended to construct curriculum with the children, I knew I couldn't plan in great detail ahead of time, but that didn't matter. As long as I grounded myself solidly in research and theory, we would work out the specifics as we went along.

.   .   .   .   .

Dear Uncle Chris,

I'd really like to meet Auntie Brenda! You'd never believe that I have 20 people in my class and the same teacher for the third time! I'm in second grade. Mom and Dad are fine. So is Jarrett. I hope you two are fine. I can't wait to see you!

Love,
Jamie

Laurie's brother, Chris, had moved to California a few years before, but was still very close to his family in Hawai'i. Jamie missed him and wrote to him often. This letter to her uncle captures better than I can how perfectly natural it felt for us to be together again. From the first day of school, I was in educational heaven. It's hard to describe. Often, children enter a new class in the fall with some trepidation. There are anxious looks, fearful silences, and sometimes tears or tantrums as they try to cope with unfamiliar surroundings and people. And it doesn't get much better for a while, because it takes time to become accustomed to new routines and expectations.

But this year was so different! It was the smoothest, most pleasant beginning I have ever encountered. The second graders and I greeted each other with hugs and smiles, ready to pick up where we had left off in June. Maybe because the festive atmosphere was so contagious, or maybe because it just seemed so normal, the new first graders seemed to blend effortlessly into the group, helped along by the older children.

Jamie was an invaluable help, working patiently, as always, with those who sought her assistance. We had a first grader, Mark, who was new to our school and whose kindergarten teacher had suggested he be monitored for possible referral to special education. Although he could converse with fluency and apparent understanding about many topics, he seemed to have limited print awareness and little interest in reading or writing. He would daydream over the blank pages in his writing folder and, when questioned, would just say he was "thinking."

Early in September, Mark noticed Jamie working busily with her books and stories, and he started watching her every day. After about a week, he began to sit next to her during our reading and writing workshops so he could watch her more closely. He started asking her about what she was writing, and she shared her work with him.

At the end of the second week, he grew brave enough to try writing on his own. Listening as unobtrusively as possible, I'd hear him ask Jamie as he worked alongside her, "How do you spell 'Mom'?" or "What letter sounds like 'sss'?" It didn't take long for him to attempt his own spelling, which opened up the whole world of writing for him. He wrote nonstop for the rest of the year.

Mark became a reader in the same way, by watching Jamie and then apprenticing himself to her. Through their collaboration, he began a yearlong passion for books. I never did refer him for special education; it wasn't necessary. I'm sure I couldn't have been as effective had I tried to "tutor" him only by myself. So often we can help children best by just getting out of their way and creating the conditions that enable them to help each other.

Writing our lives

Jamie inspired many other classmates to read and write. She was now reading chapter books, and her enthusiastic recommendations encouraged others to do the same. When her friends came to her house to visit, the first thing they did was explore her chapter book collection, which included literary classics as well as many of the popular mystery and adventure series titles.

However, Jamie's interest in books went beyond her own collection. When someone sent Laurie a set of romance novels, she put the books aside, thinking she'd look them over when she had time. A few days later, she noticed that Jamie had found the books and was deeply engrossed in them. Laurie knew that Jamie and her friends liked watching some of the television shows that were popular with teenagers, and she assumed these books were teenage love stories of a similar type. She was absolutely horrified when she opened one of the books later, after Jamie had gone to bed, and read, "His hand stroked her thigh as they kissed passionately"! These weren't the type of chapter books she'd imagined for her second grader!

But we can't shield our children from the media that bombard them. Even the youngest are caught up in the popular culture and interpret its messages in their own worldly, yet innocent, ways. Jamie was no exception, as she shows in the diary she was keeping at home:

I love Mark-Paul and I wish we could have five weeks together so we can play tag in the park and have picnics in the park under the tree and then we would kiss. When I grow up I'm going to make a book about love. I hope he would come to my house when I'm 15 and pick me up for dates and we would get married.

Jamie must have read more of those romance novels or watched more television shows along the way, because her diary musings several months later are definitely more detailed:

I had the most wonderful dream in the whole world. It was kind of romantic because it was about—well, the boy's name was Chris Matthew. He was so dreamy. We were in the same class and one day our class went on a field trip and the next day it was recess. Oh yeah, almost forgot, we were in high school.

Well anyway, it was recess and he said, "Let's go for a walk, a short one. Please." So I said, "Okay." So we went across the street and then he said, "Let's do it in my hotel room," and I said, "No, not yet, let's go slow." Then I said, "Wait till we're older, okay?"

Then this is the fun part. We French kissed five times. The day after that we went on a class trip. It was a park and it was nice and green. But after the trip was over we went home so me and Chris could stay and talk. Well, all we talked about was how we were going to work out things.

I was relieved that Jamie stuck to more conventional subjects in her school writing. It would have been hard to explain X rated authors' folders to our administrators! Her output proliferated as she began writing what she referred to as chapter books, both alone and with others. She had endless story ideas; she would be thinking of her next one even while she was working on the one in front of her. Sometimes she projected her story ideas far into the future as she did with her plan to make a book about love "when I grow up." She connected writing with everything she did; whatever was important in her real world found its way into her story world.

Jamie didn't finish all the stories she began. Sometimes she lost interest in an idea, or it didn't work out as she had hoped. Sometimes, too, she would put a partially written story aside, work on something else for a while, and return to complete her story later. All that was fine with me; that's how writers operate.

But Jamie wrote constantly, and she would persist without letup on stories that "worked" for her. She would often write 150 or 200 words a day. I would confer with her briefly as I circulated among the children during writing time, and she would share her current efforts. I showed I valued what she wrote by using her words as we discussed the story. Sometimes I'd ask her to tell me a little more about a particular incident, inquire about what she might write next, or make a similar comment that I hoped would help her focus her thoughts and keep going.

I didn't interrupt Jamie's flow of ideas with concerns about mechanics while she was composing. Editing came later, when her words were safely recorded, and it was never a chore for her, because it was done for an authentic purpose. My students knew, by virtue of many discussions and sharing sessions, that there are situations when we must write conventionally. When we write for ourselves, we can spell the words any way we wish, as long as we know what we have written. But when we write for others, we need to use accepted conventions so that our intended audience can read what we have written. Jamie wanted very much to share her stories, so editing for spelling, punctuation, and general usage was a natural part of the process. And she remembered what she learned from these editing sessions and applied them to subsequent writing.

Jamie worked on and off for two months, from October through December, on a story she called *The Sliding Rainbow*. This story incorporated many aspects of life that were significant to her, such as family, friends, fairness, and overcoming problems. It also mixed home and school, reality and fantasy, in delightful ways. Here are the first two parts, slightly edited for clarity:

Part I

Once there was a rainbow. It was in the park. Children could slide on it. They had fun sliding on it. But one day there was a storm and the rainbow blew off of the park.

The next day the rainbow did not come back. The children were sad. They didn't play all day. They just looked out the window looking at the sky.

There was a girl named Stacy. She loved the rainbow so much she cried. But one day the rainbow came back and she was happy.

Stacy told the other children that the rainbow came back, and all the children ran to the park and the rainbow was waiting. And of all the days, the children were happy and the rainbow was happy, too, and they played all day.

Part II

The next day the sliding rainbow was telling the children there was a newborn tree, the Secret Tree. It was underneath the rainbow.

"Do you know why it's called the Secret Tree? Because it grows without water." Stacy was even more happy! Stacy ran home and she told her mom about the exciting day. She went to her room and she made up a song. She sang so loud her mother could hear her.

The next day Stacy told her friend Kelly the song she made up. Kelly told Stacy an idea. The idea was: we should call the rainbow's sister so that the rainbow and her sister can play together. Stacy thought it was a good idea.

The next day Kelly called the rainbow's sister. The sister said she would come. Kelly and Stacy were happy. One hour later, the rainbow's sister came. The rainbow's sister's name was Special because she did special things. She could make the sun come and go.

When Special came to the park, the rainbow was so happy she ran to her sister. First they talked and then they played.

It was getting dark. Special had to leave. Then the rainbow had to cry. Stacy tried to cheer the rainbow up but the rainbow still cried.

The next day, the rainbow stopped crying because the rainbow made a new friend. Stacy and Kelly were happy. Sister was happy, too. But then something bad happened to the rainbow and the friend. They started fighting.

They were fighting about a jump rope. They took turns, but they pulled on it, so it broke. They called each other names. They were mad. They said, "Pumpkin Head" and "Mouse Face." They sure were mad! Kelly called their mother. She came and she scolded them.

I enjoyed Jamie's mirroring of the real-life disagreements children have, along with her use of our class's "secret tree" as a story element. We had "adopted" a tree on our school campus and would visit it often, sometimes for observation and study, and sometimes to relax and read in its welcoming shade. Because of our tree, the children had developed a personal appreciation for nature. All of the students, Jamie in particular, loved knowing this was "our" tree and keeping it our special secret. I liked the way Jamie incorporated the tree while giving it new qualities ("It grows without water"), thus making it more her own and adding to the magic of her story.

One day, Jamie told me very excitedly that she was starting a new story. She had written:

I'm going to make a new book called Wishes. It's going to be about a girl who always made wishes because she had a special unicorn that made her wishes come true. But one day she was playing in the park and she lost it and when she made wishes it didn't come true and she was really sad. But one night she had a dream that she found her unicorn! But when she woke up she was confused about if it's really true or not.

Well, the next day she went back to the park and she went to the swing and found her unicorn. But when she lifted it the horn came off and she was a little sad. When she went home she glued the horn back on. And if you want to find out what happened next, read the book.

I was a little confused, so I asked her why she had ended her story this way. She said, "It's not the story yet." She explained that this was just something to make people want to read her story, like the blurbs she read on book jackets or at the end of a book that was part of an ongoing series. I was delighted! Through her wide reading, she was internalizing aspects of books that I hadn't even thought about pointing out to the students.

The next day, Jamie started working on the story. She enlisted Cari and Annie to work with her, Cari as a plot consultant and Annie to color the illustrations she planned to make. The part of her draft below shows how Jamie was internalizing literary language as well as usage and mechanics. It is also a charming example of her reverence for all life, as she neatly plots her heroine's treatment of the worm.

Once upon a time there was a girl named Mayra and she had a necklace with a magic unicorn that made wishes come true, and when Mayra made wishes it came true except for bad ones. One day she went to the park and she lost it. "Where's my unicorn? I need to find it."

Well, for two days she was doomed. I'm serious. Well, she gave up on the next day. But on the fourth day, she went back to the park and when she went to the swing she kicked the unicorn. Then she saw it and stopped and she picked it up. But something was different. The horn came off and a little tear came running down her cheek because she knew that that was what made her wishes come true. But she found the horn in the dirt.

But she saw it moving in the dirt because a worm was moving it. So she got a stick so the worm would climb up and Mayra picked up the horn. So when she went home she glued the horn back on the unicorn.

That was Jamie, wanting always, in real life or in fiction, to resolve conflicts peacefully and without harm to anyone. Her social consciousness was expanding from her immediate surroundings to a more global view of her world. I think this came about in large part from the books and rich discussions, both at home and at school, that helped shape her awareness and values. I could see the difference in her thinking as she began expressing her concern about pollution, littering, wars, hunger, and homelessness. That year she had many opportunities to translate that concern into action.

Living our curriculum

In September 1992 a devastating hurricane struck the Hawaiian island of Kaua'i. Donations of food, clothing, and other necessities for those affected by the storm were collected all over the state and elsewhere. Our school families contributed to the local effort.

In class, we shared our feelings about the hurricane as we followed the media reports and heard from friends and relatives who were victims of the storm. We talked one day about a newspaper article that dealt with the fears and hardships faced by children whose homes had been destroyed. The article pointed out that these children had lost all their toys, a fact overlooked by many adults because they didn't consider toys to be necessities. Yet that is exactly what toys are, especially at a time when children are most in need of comfort. The article suggested donations of used toys, particularly soft, stuffed dolls and animals that could be hugged and building sets that children could use to act out their recollections and fears about the hurricane.

My class immediately wanted to help, but they decided they didn't want to limit their donations to used toys. They felt that the children of Kaua'i should have new toys, too. I asked them how they would get the money for new toys. Some just wanted to ask their parents, but I tried to dissuade them from this easy route. Finally, one child suggested we do something to earn the money, and everyone agreed.

Our next step was to figure out what we would do. Literature again came to the rescue. We had recently read a story about some children who sold lemonade to earn enough money to buy a wedding present for their teacher. Jamie and Cari whispered to each other for a few minutes and then offered, "Why don't we sell lemonade to earn the money, like the kids in the book?" Everyone was enthusiastic about the idea, so that was what we did. In fact, the lemonade project became our curriculum for the next several weeks, as we read and tested recipes, learned how to count money and give change, wrote advertisements, and planned and carried out the sale, using Lambert's puppet center as our lemonade stand. After the sale, which netted us $77, we walked to a nearby store so the children could select the toys themselves. Then we gift-wrapped the new toys, along with the used ones the children had collected, and sent them to a school on Kaua'i, with accompanying individual letters, photos, a disposable camera, and a request for pictures of the recipients.

We received wonderful, heartwarming letters and photos from the children who received the toys. We saw exactly where each of our gifts had gone. We collected the letters and our own writing about and photos of the project, and created *Our Lemonade Book,* which became a very special part of our classroom library. The children read and shared it proudly. They also continued corresponding with their new Kaua'i friends for the rest of the year.

My students were thrilled that they had learned so much and performed such a greatly appreciated service. Jamie summed it up in her evaluation of the project: "The lemonade made me happy because we made so much money. I feel proud about myself. I feel sad for Kaua'i. I felt like I was learning for a hundred years." I thought again of Kenneth and the stroller and what true self-esteem is all about. Empathizing with others is a lofty goal, but taking action as a result of that empathy is what makes a difference for us and for our world.

Jamie apparently realized this need for social action. Her concern over litter and pollution had evolved from her first-grade pledge to keep her environment clean. She now took it upon herself to try to influence others. For Earth Day in April, our class made a "talking trash can." The children took turns speaking into a hidden microphone, thoroughly enjoying the laughter and astonished looks our trash can received as it greeted passersby and reminded them to pick up litter. Again, Jamie's evaluation summed up everyone's feelings: "I think it was fun because not only do the other kids learn about it, we learn too, because if we hadn't come up with the idea then no one would learn, even us. I hope the people who learned would pass it on so those people learn not to litter. I liked when kids all came to learn."

Jamie wrote later that year of her personal wishes, and I was struck by the remarkable change from those of her kindergarten year: "Owning a toy store; no more wars; no hungry people; no more storms or hurricanes; six more wishes; no poor people; no rich people because they get greedy; and—oh yes, I forgot—I wish I could walk!"

It's ironic that while Jamie wished she could walk, others in our class wished they were in wheelchairs because "then people could carry me around, too." Children don't always look beyond the surface of a situation to think about the difficulties it might present, so Jamie's friends never realized the pain and disappointment she dealt with every day, especially when illness kept her from participating in some class activities. But she influenced others even when she wasn't there.

In February, as part of our study of stars, we had a sleepover at school. It was an exciting event. The children planned all the activities, and I helped them with the logistics. Literature played a large part in the planning. My husband, Hoyt, had visited our class a few times, and the children had enjoyed his reading aloud and storytelling. Now they decided to invite him to tell them ghost stories in the dark at our secret tree, after which we would go to our school library to read joke books so everyone would sleep well. They also invited my daughter Nani and her husband, Wesley. Nani had come to read and write with the children several times, and Wes had taken them on a tour of his business. They were now considered part of our school family, and the children wanted to share the special occasion with them.

Jamie took an active part in the planning, thinking of details that others might have missed. She worked with her small group to brainstorm the supplies each child would need to bring, and she wrote down the list. In addition to the usual items, such as clothes, toothbrushes, and

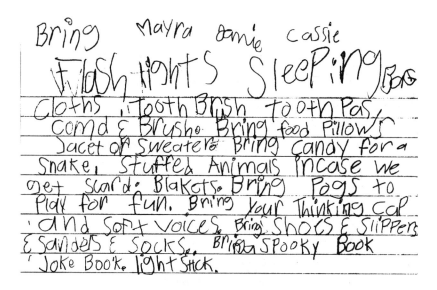

Bring Mayra Jamie cassie
Flash lights Sleeping Bas
cloths , Tooth Brush Tooth Pas,
comd & Brush. Bring food Pillows
Jacet or Sweaters Bring candy for a
Snake, Stuffed Animals incase we
get scard. Blakets. Bring Pogs to
Play for fun. Bring your Thinking cap
and Soft voices, Bring Shoes & Slippers
& Sandels & socks. Bring Spooky Book
Joke Book. light stick.

sleeping bags, Jamie contributed the following suggestions: "Stuffed animals in case we get scared . . . Bring your thinking cap and soft voices. . . . Bring a spooky book. Joke book."

Unfortunately, Jamie wasn't able to come to the sleepover. She had caught yet another of her frequent colds and was bound to the suctioning machine once again because of the mucus buildup in her lungs. Her friends missed her presence as much as she missed being there. Knowing of Jamie's love for both sending and receiving letters, some children decided to write to her and share a little of the occasion. Cari wrote:

The sleepover was fun. What did you do at home? We're sorry you couldn't come to the sleepover. . . . You probably didn't want to come 'cause Mr. Parker told spooky stories. They were true. One was about some bones that were in a tree. You could see them at night but in the day you couldn't see the bones. That is true, and that really happened to Mr. Parker.

P.S. Spooky stories were at the Secret Tree.

I thought it was cute that Cari tried to lessen Jamie's disappointment with her description of the scary story. I also marveled at the way

Jamie had helped so many others find personal value in letter writing, as she continued to do for herself.

The children thought of Jamie's wheelchair as something very special. Sometimes they wanted to try it out when she was in a different chair. Jamie enjoyed the sharing and, of course, the attention. One day, Laurie brought me a copy of a letter Jamie had written to one of her favorite television actors, Luke Perry. Jamie had read in a magazine that he welcomed letters from his fans and encouraged them to tell him about themselves.

Dear Luke Perry,

I saw you on TV. I'm in a wheelchair. My classmates and I like your TV shows. . . . I'm going to go to singing lessons, but I'm going to go when I'm older. For now, I just go to school. In school I'm popular because I'm in a wheelchair.

I was truly moved by this letter. It expresses so powerfully how far we had come from our worry two years earlier that Jamie would not be accepted by her classmates.

Singing lessons were in Jamie's plan for the not-too-distant future. In addition, she was starting to think about her long-term educational and career goals. Throughout the year, she had been saying she wanted to be an author, and maybe an illustrator too. This was her strongest desire, but she also developed other interests.

In December, our class began a sustained inquiry into geology. At that time, my daughter Jennifer was majoring in geology at the University of Hawai'i. Auntie Jennifer became our special resource person, visiting and helping us whenever she could. Her expertise, enthusiasm, and ability to work well with children hooked many of them into wanting to know more. They loved learning and trying some of the things that real geologists do.

As part of our study, we took an after-school trip to the university's geology department, where the children took part in geology activities prepared just for us. It was the first time some of the parents who accompanied us had been on the university campus. It was perhaps the first time many of the children realized there is a place called a university where they might be able to go someday if they worked and studied hard. Not all parents have been to college, nor do they necessarily see college as a possibility for their children. I'm not saying everyone has to go to college, but everyone should know it's an option within their reach. Our university trip taught me that it's never too early to have children know this. It's important to have long-term goals for our lives, even though they might change many times, and I encouraged the children to think about such things.

The close relationship Jamie was developing with Jennifer, along with her fascination with rocks, led her to decide she now wanted to become an author *or a geologist*. She began to collect rocks and to talk more with Jen about the kinds of things geologists do. She was happy to learn that not all geologists have to do field work; she would be able to do laboratory work in her wheelchair.

Jamie brought several of her most colorful rocks to school to share with the class. The children were awed by their beauty and mystery, and they spent hours with our reference books as they attempted to identify and learn more about each one. Rocks became the treasures of our classroom, objects of wonder, the focus of our reading and writing, and even a catalyst for social interaction.

In our class, as in many others, there was a friendly rivalry between the boys and the girls. They liked each other and teased each other at the same time. Whenever we read any type of trickster tale, I could safely predict that a rash of tricks would follow, as the children sought to outdo each other with their creativity. I didn't mind as long as the tricks didn't hurt anyone or interfere with their learning, because they were done with a sense of humor, not with any meanness of spirit.

The rock trick was probably the most elaborate. The boys were fascinated with the origins of Jamie's shiny rock specimens, and Jamie, Mayra, Annie, Cari, and Jamilee decided it would be fun to make the boys think they had found a valuable rock right on our school campus. Their plan was truly a collaborative effort. They found a small plain rock outside and stayed in secretly at recess for the next few days to cover it with several layers of glue and multicolored glitter. (It looked pretty authentic if you didn't look too closely.)

When the rock was completely dry, they sneaked it back outside and hid it behind some bushes near our room. During the next recess, they instigated a game of chase that just "happened" to lead the boys to the bushes, where they "discovered" the rock. The boys came running back to our room in great excitement to tell about their marvelous find, and they didn't catch on to the joke until some time later. They laughed as hard as the girls did when they found out.

Looking back, I think these tricks furthered our sense of community. They added an indefinable yet unmistakable spirit to the classroom and became a part of our shared history. As a family, we were living our curriculum, building the memories that would shape and define us and that we would treasure in times to come.

Learning from learners

Even with all the geology excitement, we were still immersed in reading and in our literature study groups. But I decided to try some changes in the children's reading homework. I still asked parents to read to their children daily, but I didn't require the reader-response journals. Instead I designed a new homework log, which included an invitation and space for parents to write their comments and questions about the shared reading. In addition, I asked the children to keep their own reader-response journals in school, hoping they would help each other with their writing.

Jamie's written responses to literature were usually brief but always refreshing. They were further documentation of her thoughtful appreciation of stories. Her wide and varied reading gave her a solid foundation to build on as she encountered new stories. She often compared and connected books:

> *Petunia is a helpful and funny duck at the same time. I think Petunia and Morris the Moose* [Morris Goes to School] *are like twins, because they're both animals and they're both funny and they both could not count.*

> *I think Bunnicula is a vampire because I compared the garlic part of the story to what happened to a lady in another story. The lady came to a door where another lady was cooking with garlic and she came still. So did Bunnicula.*

Stories always triggered Jamie's curiosity and sense of wonder. Her reflections on literature usually included new questions she thought of as she read, so she began dividing her journal pages in half vertically, labeling the left column *Wonderside* and using the right column to record other responses to the text (for humorous stories, she labeled this column *Funnyside*). Here are some examples:

The Boxcar Children

Wonderside	*Funnyside*
I wonder what happened when they went back to the mainland? I wonder how old Jessie and Henry and Violet and Benny were?	*I like when Benny hollered.*

My Father's Dragon

Wonderside	*Funnyside*
I wonder why the dragon flew with his sore wing? I wonder if it got better?	*I think it was funny when the animals were on top of the alligators.*

When Jamie read a book she particularly enjoyed, she always noted that she wished the author would write a sequel. That may explain why she wrote so many sequels to her own stories. She wrote as a reader; she read as a writer.

Although this new reader-response procedure was working reasonably well, I missed the parent-child journals of the previous two years. Jamie's mother missed them too. Even with a busier schedule at home (Lambert was working on a construction project some distance away and was able to be home only on weekends for several months), Laurie kept faithfully to the reading, her belief in its value unwavering. She was so used to writing her thoughts in great detail that she couldn't abandon the process. She was cramming so many words into the small comment spaces on the log sheets that I included blank sheets with Jamie's folder so Laurie could write more. Our dialogue continued all year, and I will always be grateful that it did. I could hardly wait to read each day's entry! Through word and example, Laurie was teaching me how her family was extending and expanding Jamie's literacy development.

Research indicates that children construct meaning from a text in light of their own experiences and by talking with others about what they've read. Literature experiences like this make comprehension questions unnecessary. Meaningful interactions with books uncover multilayered story elements far beneath the surface plot and enable readers to reach a deeper understanding and to connect the story to their lives (Harste et al. 1988; Peterson and Eeds 1990; Short and Pierce 1990).

I saw this happening with Jamie and Laurie. Early in Jamie's kindergarten year, when the journals began, Laurie's entries were mostly plot synopses. By the end of first grade, they dealt increasingly with life, family and personal values, and a broadening worldview. Now in second grade I saw another dramatic leap: more in-depth explorations, more critical reading, and greater understanding.

There were still constant connections with Jamie's personal life, family, and values:

This book, <u>Barry: the Bravest Saint Bernard</u>, brought on a LOT of conversation. First of all, [Jamie] told me about the movie she saw with her daddy called <u>Beethoven</u>. It was about a dog who was a Saint Bernard. Second, she told me about a TV movie about the musician Beethoven. She said he was deaf and could play good music and that his father was strict. And third, we talked about what we'd discovered about monks, the monastery, about their duties up in the mountains, about bravery, honesty, and trust, about how dogs and humans age, etc. I read to her while she was bathing and we discussed almost every page. The book covers a lot of territory!

We also discussed our own morals and values and spiritual beliefs. It was quite in-depth. I told Jamie that we shared so much and it's amazing how one book can bring so much thought. She said it's called connec-

tions! One thought brings other thoughts! . . . What a nice, long, informative bath!!

> *We looked at the picture of the dog, Angus, and it reminded us of Annie's pet dog. . . . Jamie pointed out that she knew how Angus felt when his friend, the cat, couldn't be found. She said she feels lonely when Jarrett plays at his friend's house on Saturdays and she has no brother. Angus and the cat fought, too, just like Jamie and her brother. But Jamie said she misses him even if they fight.*
>
> *Jamie and I also thought of Grandma Lo. She had a dog named Noi and a cat named Maui Girl. Jamie had fond memories, and even remembered a time when Maui Girl's kitten scratched her finger. Ouch! I suggested to Jamie that she share the book, <u>Angus and the Cat</u>, with Grandma Lo one day. She was kind of worried that Grandma would feel sad because Noi passed away and Maui Girl was lost and never found.*
>
> *Jamie and I also noticed the copyright was 1931, and Jamie seemed really surprised. She wondered if the author was still alive. We guessed if she were alive, she would be in her 80s. Jamie laughed at the fact that her Grandma Lo was about a year old at the time the book was published. It was a very nice story!*

Jamie also related stories to things that happened in school:

> <u>Ant Cities</u> *was very informative. The part Jamie and I really liked was that the queen doesn't tell her workers what to do. The workers each have a job to do. They work together to build the ant city. Just like her class. The substitute teachers don't have to tell the kids much. Each student has his/her job to do and they carry their jobs out well! They are all very independent and yet can work together very well!*

Jamie and Laurie were now also regularly exploring story themes. I hadn't assigned this; Laurie seemed to encourage it naturally, beginning in early November and continuing throughout the year. From early April, it was an integral part of nearly every discussion. I found this progression compelling evidence of what I had read in the research, that literary elements will emerge through meaningful discourse:

I read <u>Good Neighbors</u> to Jamie and she said being good to your neighbors means giving them their private time. She understood the theme of the story.

<u>Play it Again, Rosie</u> was about a girl who doesn't know until she tries. This is what Jamie said to her dad when he asked her what she just read. We all talked about fear, failure, practice makes perfect, not being afraid of making a mistake, etc. We also talked about Jarrett picking orchestra as an elective. He wants to learn to play the violin.

<u>No Elephants Allowed</u> was a story about courage. I was quite surprised Jamie used that word. I asked her if she knew what it meant, just to be sure. She did!

As their experiences with literature were broadening, Jamie and Laurie began interpreting the books more critically, not hesitating to form their own opinions. This was great! It's a quality we want to instill in all readers. We shouldn't accept anything we read at face value; we always need to think about what we are reading and draw our own thoughtful conclusions.

When they read *Leo, the Late Bloomer*, Laurie wrote:

It was interesting. While Jamie and I understood about Leo being late in learning to read, write, draw, and talk compared to his other friends, we both came up with the idea that his parents could have helped Leo instead of just watching him blossom. Jamie said his animal friends who knew all of the above things should have offered to help Leo learn to read. I explained that maybe Leo could appreciate some encouragement and even though he can't be forced to read like his friends, they could have done things with Leo and let him observe. Cute story, but I think some more pages could be added to this particular story. That's just my opinion and Jamie's, too!

Another thought just came to mind. Some parents who read this story might say to themselves, See, just let him/her blossom on his own time, but I think encouragement and even some participation would have added nicely to this story. It needs a modern version.

Laurie's opinion of *Road Robber* was more favorable:

I read it to Jamie and her dad and we all were happily surprised to see a boy in a wheelchair in the illustrations. We always get excited when we come across book illustrations that depict kids with special needs. It's especially refreshing when these kids or adults are part of the "regular" crowd and not really the main story line. We like seeing this happening in TV commercials . . . and in advertising.

Sometimes Jamie and Laurie learned new words or facts in the context of the story:

As for the book <u>Creature Features</u>, what an eye-opener for us adults. I couldn't believe it was nonfiction because we couldn't believe a spider has eight eyes, a worm has none, and a caterpillar has twelve! When Jamie first read it to us and we had to guess the creature, we thought it was funny and make-believe.

As the variety of books they read increased, Jamie and Laurie discovered new purposes for reading and new topics of interest. Many of the nonfiction books they were now reading gave them the opportunity to explore special projects, which they could then share with family and friends:

<u>*Springtime Surprises*</u>*! What a neat book! We're thinking of buying one for ourselves, or Jamie will keep reborrowing the book. We plan to make some of the creations before Easter. Jarrett and Jamie had the best time viewing the creations together and getting excited over their favorites. A lot of the materials are inexpensive and readily available.*

<u>*Mickey's Magnet*</u> *made Jamie want to try out Jarrett's little magnet. Out of all the items we tried, the magnet picked up the paper clip and a spoon. It clung to a big, heavy lock that was too heavy to lift.*

Jamie loved her books, and her family seemed caught up in her enthusiasm and enjoyment. As before, playfulness, humor, and "humanness" played a large part in their interactions:

Jamie was getting a little irritated because of Mom interrupting, so while reading a particular page, instead of "five fat monkeys," she read it as "five fat mommies." The rest of the family just laughed at her expression and Mom apologized.

Jamie's been home resting from a touch of the flu and we were probably getting on each other's nerves. She wanted to read <u>Are You My Mother?</u> She asked me in her sarcastic way, "Can you bring me the book <u>Are You My Crazy Mother?</u>" We waited until we were okay with each other again before we read together. Reading is not a "chore," but becomes fun and well received, when the mood is right.

In <u>How to Deal With Friends,</u> Jamie could relate to everything. She said it reminded her about how her friends fight and play. They sometimes fight over being field trip partners, who to sit next to at lunch, etc. They enjoy playing together, and yet Jamie also enjoys doing things by herself, too. She loves her friends and also loves making new friends. I reminded Jamie that her brother, Jarrett, could also be considered her friend. She thought a while and could relate to the "friends cheat when playing hide and seek" part.

Throughout the years Jamie was in my class, Laurie intuitively supported her as an emergent reader and encouraged her to use good reading strategies. I emphasized that what Laurie was doing was important. I also loaned her books about literacy. This two-way communication helped us both grow. Laurie's notes helped me learn more about how she was helping Jamie to be a reader, and my feedback helped Laurie feel she was moving in the right direction and encouraged her to keep going. Sometimes I would offer support for a specific strategy I observed; other times, my comments would be more general. Always, we were both excited about what we saw happening.

But I never told Laurie what to do next: I never knew what that would be. Instead, I trusted that her intuition and the natural process would help her find her way. I fully expected to learn from Laurie, and I wasn't disappointed. She continued to do the very things I thought were most helpful for Jamie and that were certainly most helpful to me. By making explicit what she did with Jamie, Laurie enabled me to look more closely at those strategies and make sure they were a part of what I did with my class.

It's crucial to build on what children already know and allow them to pursue their own way of finding meaning without belittling their efforts and approximations. Laurie seemed to be aware of this. She honored Jamie's style and language, letting Jamie enjoy the books in her own way and not imposing adult language or structure on their reading experiences.

Throughout the process, Laurie reflected often on the growth she saw in Jamie's literacy. I felt extremely fortunate that Laurie shared her thoughts so willingly. These journals traced not just one child's literacy journey, but an entire family's journey. Jamie's family had moved far beyond helping her fulfill her homework assignments, and they had been enriched by it. They found books more and more important in their lives, and they shared their love of books with others:

Jamie said that our family reads a lot. It was neat one evening because Jamie stopped and said, "Hey, look, we're all reading!" Dad, newspaper; Mom, Bible; Jarrett, book project; and Jamie, a chapter book!

This was the night Jamie read <u>When I Was Young in the Mountains</u> and we shared that story with everyone in our house. The pastor from our church and his wife and another couple were over. I reminded them I had to read with Jamie and discuss the book for homework. I excused myself and went to the back room with the kids.

While reading, we came across some unfamiliar words and we thought of our pastor's family, since we knew they were from the mountains of Tennessee. We brought the book to the front and asked them to help Jamie out with her journal. They were more than happy to participate.

Page by page we discussed the story, and it brought fond memories. They could relate to every single page, especially the illustrations. They explained to us the words that were unfamiliar. It was a pleasant experi-

ence for everyone. We all learned that sharing a story together is fun for adults and children.

As Jamie's family grew closer, so did our school family. None of the many visitors who came to our classroom could tell who were the first graders and who were the second graders. We had pretty much forgotten ourselves!

We were tied to one another and to the numerous members of our extended family who had shared in our activities throughout the year, grandparents and other relatives included. We always had at least seven adults with us on our field trips (thirteen participated in the sleepover!). Sometimes Jamie would bring her Grandpa Lo so he would know what we were studying. Relatives from other places joined us, too. Jamie's Uncle Chris and Auntie Brenda visited from California and accompanied us on one of our field trips. Jamie was delighted that they were able to become a part of her school life, and so were they.

Our closeness made parting in June especially difficult; I knew this time there would be no reprieve. I'd have to send all the children on to a new class. We all agreed, though, that we would stay in close touch. We would always be an 'Ohana.

Third Grade

Facing the challenge

So far Jamie's frequent illnesses had not become full-blown secondary infections. But her respiratory problems were worsening as she grew. She caught colds more frequently, and each one seemed to last a little longer than the one before. Since the risk of further problems would increase as the spinal curvature became more pronounced, Jamie's doctors felt it was time for corrective surgery. They recommended spinal fusion, which meant inserting a steel rod vertically into Jamie's spine in order to keep it straight. This would only be effective if it was done while Jamie was young and still growing.

Laurie and Lambert knew that surgery always involves risk and that in Jamie's case the risk was greater than average. But they also knew that doing nothing was a far greater risk in the long run and that the surgery, if successful, would give Jamie the best, perhaps the only, possibility for a normal life span. They discussed the options with their doctors and with Jamie, believing that she should have a voice in the decisions. She chose the surgery, which was scheduled to be performed the summer before she entered third grade.

Laurie and Lambert discussed the surgery with me optimistically in spite of their many misgivings. I marveled at their strength, especially since Lambert hadn't yet fully recovered from the major back surgery he'd had in April.

Jamie's surgery, which took place in July, was successful, and her recovery proceeded normally for the first twenty-four hours. On the second day, however, complications arose, and she remained in intensive care, hooked up to a ventilator and innumerable monitors. Laurie and Lambert were with her literally around the clock. Grandma Lo and other relatives took care of Jarrett and filled in at the hospital.

At the time of Jamie's surgery Hoyt and I were away visiting my mom, who was ill. As soon as we got home, we went to the hospital. I will never forget how tiny Jamie looked in the huge bed, and so helpless. She couldn't move on her own and had to remain in a very awkward position on her side, her legs sticking up spider fashion. Her long hair had been cut short so it wouldn't interfere with all the tubes and wires.

And there were so many tubes and wires! They were attached to nearly every part of her body, including her toes. Her front teeth had been extracted to make room for the ventilator tube, which filled her mouth and made it impossible for her to speak. She was hot and uncomfortable; she wore only a diaper and got little relief from the wet cloths placed on her stomach and forehead.

I had all I could do to pretend to be cheerful. How could Jamie endure the pain and discomfort? I couldn't even endure seeing her this way. I nearly lost my composure completely when she looked up and silently mouthed, "How's your mom?" That was so like Jamie, still thinking of others in the midst of her own suffering.

Jamie was extremely unhappy and frustrated during much of her time in intensive care, often displaying visible anger, especially toward the physical therapists who had to give her necessary but painful chest therapy. She pulled out her ventilator and other tubes several times, causing further complications; eventually her hands had to be put in restraints. When a hospital counselor asked her to indicate her feelings on paper, she circled *confused*, *afraid*, *sad*, and *angry*. She had little interest in the toys and stuffed animals that people brought her. Sometimes she would listen to stories read to her, although she couldn't hold the books to read by herself. But nothing seemed to distract her for very long, understandably so. The one thing that seemed to give her some comfort was a favorite rock; she would lie there clutching it tightly. Hoyt and I visited Jamie often, wishing we could do something more but feeling helpless.

I realize now that Jamie's frustration didn't stem primarily from her physical problems; she had dealt with pain and discomfort all her life. But before she had been able to talk and write about her feelings; now she could do neither. She was cut off from all means of normal communication with others, and that loss, to her, was unbearable. Somehow she sensed that and decided to do something about it.

One morning, Jamie began making indecipherable gestures with her hands. After some trial-and-error guesswork, Laurie realized that Jamie wanted paper and something to write with. A nurse found some computer paper and pens, and Jamie wrote by holding both paper and pen in the air. The letters were shaky, but the message was clear: "I want a cup of ice." She got her ice immediately.

And so began Jamie's self-liberation. She finally had an outlet for her frustration and a viable way to communicate her needs and desires, and her mood lightened a bit. In her awkward position she couldn't write much, but it was enough to make her physical and emotional needs known: "I want some water." "I want a wet cloth." "I want to go on my back." "If you can, I want to watch a video." "Stay here, please." "I want my dad." "I can't sleep because I don't have my mom." "When you talk about Cari you make me homesick." Being able to respond to her requests left everyone feeling a bit less helpless; we could do something, however small, to make things better.

Jamie was used to communicating openly and participating in all family decisions and events, including those involving her medical situation. In the hospital she felt left out. Not only did the doctors and nurses exclude her from the discussions they held at her bedside, they sometimes seemed to forget she was there. As soon as Jamie had access to paper, she wrote: "Could you turn my bed so I can see you have your meetings?" From then on, the doctors made sure she was able to see and interact with them as they conferred.

With her paper and pen, Jamie could become more involved in what was going on around her and take part in conversations, no matter how brief. Her sense of isolation decreased.

Here's my favorite example of Jamie's hospital writing. Because mucus constantly collected in her lungs, her doctors ordered physical

Stay here
Please

I want my
Dad & Jarrex

Can I Have
a Bath

I can't
relax

therapy as needed. One morning, Jamie felt unusually congested when she woke up. A doctor wasn't due for several hours, but Jamie didn't have to wait. She wrote: "I feel like I need a chest PT," and the nurses called the physical therapist. Later, when the doctor arrived and read her chart, he asked in great surprise, "Who ordered the chest PT?" The nurses delightedly reported that Jamie had ordered it herself!

Laurie and Lambert saved every page Jamie wrote in the hospital, finding comfort in knowing that her writing was of such great personal use to her. This unique "journal" is the most authentic use of writing I've ever seen. Jamie was using her literacy to empower herself in ways I'd never imagined.

Jamie remained in intensive care for two agonizing months and was then transferred to Shriners Hospital for Crippled Children for a few weeks of rehabilitation to prepare her for going home. She was a little happier at Shriners, mostly because she was able to attend daily classes at the hospital "school," a transitional program for recuperating patients who would soon be returning to their own schools.

In late September, Jamie was finally discharged from the hospital. She was still very weak, but the doctors were hopeful that time and extensive physical therapy would contribute to her full recovery. She would not be able to return to school for at least several more months, but when she became a little stronger, she could have a home tutor.

Jamie missed school and longed to be with her classmates again. But now they could at least visit her, and she could talk with them on the phone. Laurie overheard Jamie and one of her friends reminiscing on the phone one day about their experiences in our 'Ohana class—in the "olden days," as they put it. They missed each other terribly.

Sadly, Jamie's recovery at home was slow and painful. Her lungs had never fully cleared after the surgery, and she had to return to the hospital several times.

But by November Jamie was a little stronger; it was time for the home tutor. Laurie and Lambert wanted someone Jamie already knew and liked. By a happy coincidence, my daughter Nani was available and most willing to take the job. Jamie was thrilled that Auntie Nani would be her tutor and her link with the outside world.

Jamie and Nani had an excellent relationship. Nani was told she could be flexible about how she and Jamie "covered" the material sent home by the third-grade teachers. Most of it consisted of worksheets and spelling and vocabulary lists—things of little interest to Jamie, although she could do them with ease as long as someone helped her fill them out, since her arms and hands were weaker than ever.

So Nani and Jamie breezed through the worksheets as quickly as possible in order to allow time for the "fun stuff"—meaningful conversations about literature and almost every subject imaginable. As Nani said, "Mostly we just talked."

Usually these discussions were prompted by Jamie: she would mention something she was curious about and Nani would find resources to help her learn more about it. These inquiries took diverse, often unexpected, turns. For example, they talked a lot about Jamie's concern for the ways disabled people are portrayed in the media; in that context she became interested in learning about Stephen Hawking. Nani brought in some books by and about Hawking, which they read and discussed together for several days.

Nani's journal of her experiences with Jamie describes the way they worked together. Here are a few examples:

One thing I noticed about Jamie's math learning is that sometimes she hesitated to answer questions that involved filling in the blanks, such as the following on a worksheet:

$$10 - 6 = 4$$
$$10 - 4 = 6$$
$$\_\_ + \_\_ = 10$$

When I asked her why she didn't answer this type of problem right away, she said, "Well, NOW I think I was supposed to put 6 and 4 or 4 and 6. But when I looked at it I was thinking the answer could be a lot of things. It could be 5 and 5 or 7 and 3 or 10 and 0." So we discussed the idea of supplying the most obvious answer and then she completed the problem set.

[My response to this entry is, Hooray! She's *thinking,* not just filling in blanks!]

Another thing about Jamie's reading is that she notices everything, even the illustrations. In the story about the talking leaves she told me that the illustrations of Sequoyah didn't show him in what she thought was Native American clothes. One drawing depicting him with his children looked like it could be a traditional American Indian outfit, but the drawing at the end (with something that resembles a turban) she thought looked "not right." So I found a book that has a lot of archival photos and photos of artifacts. Jamie found the Cherokee listed in the group of Southeast tribes. Then she found photos of artifacts, including clothing of Southeast tribes. She successfully used two different identification keys to identify the objects and what tribal groups used them. I asked her how she figured out how to use the identification keys and she said she watched her brother using some in a similar type of book. Jamie found photos of Indians wearing garb similar to that worn in the illustrations of Sequoyah, but they were of two different tribes, neither of them Cherokee!

Nani was amazed that she could talk with Jamie in the same way she talked with her adult colleagues and that she and Jamie learned so much from each other. She found Jamie a delightful mix of child and grownup: "She could be a little kid one minute, playing make-believe, but then in the next minute we could talk like adults. She was wise beyond her years." They enjoyed their time together so much that Nani's one hour a day often stretched to three or more.

Jamie liked having Nani eat breakfast or lunch with her, and she would eat more when Nani was there. But she still ate relatively little, which was worrisome; she seemed to be getting weaker. And as she weakened, she ate less and grew weaker still. By December, she was back in the hospital with yet another recurrence of pneumonia.

Shortly before Christmas, Jamie's doctors told her family what they had hoped they wouldn't hear: her respiratory system was failing and her weight was much too low. There were options, and there were dangers. They could perform an operation to insert a feeding tube, but another surgery, given Jamie's greatly weakened condition, would be even more risky than the previous one, and at best it would probably do nothing more than buy her a few extra months. Or they could do nothing and let nature take its course. In that case, she might have as few as nine months left to live.

Laurie and Lambert had known from the time Jamie was first diagnosed in infancy that she might not live to adulthood. But knowing something intellectually doesn't prepare you for dealing with it emotionally. And what about Jamie's role in the decisions to be made? Summoning all their strength and courage, they again decided that Jamie had the right to take an active part in those decisions.

Jamie proved to be the strongest of all. She told her family that she didn't want to go through any more surgery. She wanted no more tubes, no more wires, and no more intensive care units. She knew her body was weakening, and she was ready to accept the inevitable, as long as she could be with her family and friends in reasonable comfort. Jamie was discharged from the hospital to spend her last Christmas at home.

On the surface, she carried on as if everything were quite normal. On December 22, she and Cari wrote me a cheerful letter:

Dear Mrs. Parker,

Hi! I just wanted to say hi from me and Cari because Cari was at my house December 22 at night. She's helping me think of what to say. I'm practicing my school homework very, very hard. I can't wait to go back to school. So does Cari too. Well, gotta go. Bye. See you soon, I hope.

Love,
Jamie and Cari

12/22/93

Dear mrs. Parker,
   Hi! I just wanted to Say hi
from me and Cari because Cari was
at my house December 22 at night.
She's helping me think of What to
Say. I'm practicking my Shcool homewrk
very, very hard. I can't Wait to go back
to Shcool So does Cari too. Well gotta go
Bye See you soon I hope.

Love,
Jamie & Cari

Was she trying to shield us from the truth, or did her words help her deal with it? She was well aware of her situation, yet she still held on to a thread of hope and longing as she wrote a poignant letter to Santa:

To Mr. Santa Claus,

If you really are Santa, I just want you to tell God I want a longer life to live. That's all I want, just a longer life to live. No toys and that's it.

Love,
Your friend,
Jamie Panui

P.S. If you can, I just want to say thanks and I believe you can do it.

to mr. Santa claus,
If you really are santa I
Just What you to tell God.
I what a longer life to live
that's all I what Just a
longer life to live no toys
& that's it.

Love
Your Friend
Jamie Panui

P. S. If you can I Just
want to say thanks. & I
belive you can do it.

Laurie and Lambert were faced with having to create a festive atmosphere in the midst of their sadness. Family and friends gathered for the holiday, and Jamie loved having them there. She was too weak to be more than an onlooker, but she was still able to enjoy the books they brought and read to her. A few days after Christmas, she returned to the hospital, this time to her own room. There would be no more intensive care units.

Sharing our gifts

Jamie's room during her first weeks back in the hospital was filled with activity. Relatives and friends came and went, bringing as much good cheer and laughter as they could muster. Chris and Brenda flew back from California to spend as much time with her as they could. Some of her classmates came, too. At the beginning, Jamie could still laugh with them, and she loved having company. She had her prized rock collection with her and spent hours teaching the hospital staff and visitors about each rock. She also enjoyed sharing photo albums from our 'Ohana class and her earlier years in school. I asked her one day if she would like me to bring our class lemonade book so she could share it, too, and she agreed enthusiastically. It was one of her favorites.

It always amazed us to see how many people were drawn to Jamie. People who knew her only slightly, or who had only heard of her, came to visit. Friends of friends, former classmates of Laurie and Lambert, new and old acquaintances, came together in that hospital room. They always left with more than they had brought. The strength and love they found there was a magnet, pulling them back again and again.

Jamie's Uncle Monty, who lived in Japan, came to see her. Because Monty lived so far away, she hadn't been able to share her school activities with him in a very detailed way, and she wanted to make up for lost time. My students keep notebooks filled with all the poems and songs they've learned during the year, reading and singing from them daily and taking them home to keep when the year is over. Jamie still had her song books from the past three years, and she proudly taught Monty every song in every book. I was delighted that she was still deriving so much pleasure from these books, and Monty was impressed that she remembered everything in them!

Jamie's cousin Danelle, still a student herself, knew how much Jamie had enjoyed writing. Now that Jamie could no longer keep her own journal, Danelle decided to make one and keep it for her. She recorded a few sentences each day, a gesture of love that moved us all.

Sending and receiving letters had always been an important part of Jamie's life. She couldn't write anymore, but she was still inspiring others to write to her, and the letters and cards she received adorned her wall. I was especially touched by one letter, from a girl she hardly knew:

> You may not know who I am, but I do know who you are. I'm part of the teen group at church. I just wanted to say thanks because whether or not you know it, you give me strength through your strength. You see, I play soccer and I get tired during really tough games. But when I feel like walking instead of running or not trying my best, I think of you and the pain you go through, and a fire starts burning inside of me. And guess what? I stop feeling sorry for myself and I try harder! You're my inspiration during times like these. I really admire your spunk and faith, and I'm proud of you—because you don't give up. . . . I thank God for you because you've touched so many people's lives in a positive way, including mine.

I thought often during those days about the power of literacy in our lives. Reading and writing were so strongly a part of Jamie that they were able to sustain her during those last stages of her illness. Her love of the written word was returned to her over and over again by all the people who loved her, through their letters and the books they shared with her.

In the early weeks Jamie was still able to read, and she most often asked for mystery stories and joke books. Later, when she was too weak to hold the books herself, she still wanted people to read to her. People knew how she loved books and brought her new ones every day. Even her doctors gave her books. Those last weeks are a blur of images, but the one that stands out most strongly, and that I will most remember, is Jamie lying in her bed surrounded by books. Books had wonderfully enriched her life. Being a reader goes far beyond just knowing how to read, and Jamie was a reader in every sense of the word.

Hoyt and I were at the hospital nearly every day, and Nani came often. (Jennifer was in graduate school on the mainland but kept in touch with cards and letters.) It was torture to watch Jamie grow weaker and so unbelievably thin; her legs were no bigger around than my wrists. Her weight had slipped to less than twenty pounds. Because she had so little body fat, her bones pressed painfully against the mattress, and the nurses installed a special air-cushioned one to try to alleviate some of her distress. Hoyt massaged her legs often, transferring some of his energy to her as he brought her some relief. She always received this gift with a most grateful smile, no matter how weak she was.

During the final weeks Jamie was given morphine, which she self-administered by pressing a button. It helped to see her more comfortable, even as we knew the end was getting closer. Finally, her breathing became even more labored, and she was placed on oxygen. But, as she had wished, there was no ventilator tube; instead, she had a small plastic mask, which didn't seem to bother her too much, and which made her breathing relatively easier.

Even during those last days, Jamie still wanted to be a part of things. She always asked visitors to move where she could see them. But by the last week of January, she became too weak even to talk. We thought she had slipped into a coma, but the doctors explained that she was still conscious, just too tired to respond. But her eyes still followed the activity in the room until even that movement became too difficult for her. She slept more and more. Sometimes, though, she talked in her sleep. Once Lambert heard her say, very distinctly, "Save the Earth." He said he could feel her urgency, that this was important to her.

Two days before Jamie died, a friend dropped by my classroom to visit. Marion had visited our 'Ohana class regularly as a volunteer story-teller, but we had since been out of touch. Now, hearing about Jamie and knowing of Jamie's great love for books, Marion thought of a last gift. She came to the hospital that night with a basket of books and sat by Jamie's bedside, reading and telling stories to her for two hours. Jamie couldn't respond, but we all knew she was listening. It was a sad yet beautiful time. It reaffirmed my belief that stories are not for practicing skills; they are precious gifts to be shared!

Laurie and Lambert were so moved by Marion's visit that they suggested she talk with the hospital's volunteer coordinator. Marion became the first regular volunteer storyteller for the hospital's pediatric patients. Laurie and Lambert were grateful that in this way Jamie's literacy would continue to spread to others.

We talked often during those last days about the joy Jamie had found in her reading and writing and about the comfort her family was now able to find because of it. Laurie told me how thankful she was they would always have Jamie's journals and stories. She said they would be the only things she would take with her if there was a fire or a hurricane. (I can't imagine her being thankful to have Jamie's worksheets!)

I admired the way Jamie's family accepted what was happening to her. I knew Jamie had accepted it herself. She had told her parents over and over that she knew she was dying but that she would be fine and they shouldn't worry about her. It was as the girl from Jamie's church said: through her strength, she helped to keep them strong. But I had great difficulty coming to terms with it myself. I felt anger along with my grief. Jamie was only eight years old. She loved life so much, and she had so much to look forward to! She would have made enormous contributions in her life, as a geologist, an author, or anything else. It was unfair for her to be taken from us when she had only begun to live! I didn't want her stories, and all the promise they represented, to die with her.

Then one day an answer came. If Jamie couldn't remain here to share her stories, maybe I could do it for her; I could help her be the author she had always wanted to be.

That night I knelt by her bedside, holding her hand and crying. I told her, "Jamie, I know you always wanted to be an author, and I want you to know that you *are* a real author. I've saved all your wonderful

stories, and I promise I'll write them for you so everyone can read them."
She couldn't answer, but she opened her eyes and looked into mine, and I
knew she had heard me. I also knew that I would keep that promise, for
Jamie had a great lesson to teach.

On January 29, 1994, family and close friends were called to the
hospital to say our good-byes. Nearly forty people were there. Some of
the doctors and nurses who had grown close to the family stayed when
their shifts ended. Jamie's church family sang her favorite hymns, filling
the room with the music from their hearts, their final gift. There were
tears and laughter, sorrow and joy, at the same time. Through it all,
Jamie lay surrounded by her books, her rocks, and the love of those who
knew her. She was ready, and we had to let her go.

Late in the evening, we left her with just her immediate family. She
took her last breath at 11:50 P.M. She was at peace.

Saying good-bye

Laurie and Lambert had many things to take care of during the next several days—funeral arrangements, accommodations for relatives who were coming from far away—but they were still concerned about Jamie's school family. Jamie's classmates had known she was seriously ill; she hadn't been able to attend school all year. Many had visited, called, and written to her during the past several months. But how can you prepare young children for the death of a classmate? And how do you tell them about it after it has happened?

Laurie and Lambert decided they should be the ones to tell Jamie's friends. They talked with a counselor about what they could say to the children and how they could say it. On the day they came to school, my principal hired a substitute teacher for my classroom so I could join them. I was grateful that he understood my need to be there. Jarrett was excused from his school so he could be with us too.

We would have preferred to meet with all of Jamie's former class-mates but we didn't want to disrupt the departmentalized third-grade schedule too much. The third-grade teachers hadn't known Jamie, hadn't been through our experiences, and could not really understand or appreciate our situation. We compromised by gathering together the ten children who had been closest to Jamie; we met under our secret tree, along with our school counselors.

I don't know how Laurie and Lambert did it. In the midst of their grief, they said all the right things. They told the children of Jamie's illness in terms that wouldn't frighten them. They told how important school and her friends had been to her. We cried and laughed as we remembered the good times together. We stayed under the tree through recess, until lunchtime; no one wanted to leave. The children asked if we could eat lunch together, so we agreed.

We ended up spending the entire day together. We were like any grieving family, clinging to each other for support as we dealt with our loss. We talked a lot, about Jamie, about our own feelings, and also about everyday events. Finally, Annie said, "I think I want to write a letter to Jamie," and everyone decided to do the same. My eyes filled with tears again as the children read what they wrote and I remembered Jamie's letter to Dr. Seuss so long ago:

Dear Jamie,

You are my favorite friend so I'll never forget you.
Roses are red, violets are blue,
Every day I'll care for you!!!!
Roses are red, violets blue,
When I look at the sky
I remember you!!!!!

Love,
Cari

Jamie, remember the time that me and you were helping each other with the homework? Jamie, are you brave enough to die? Jamie, I miss you very much. I'll pray for you every night. . . . Jamie, how does it feel in heaven? I miss you. I love you.

Love,
Annie

So many letters flowed to and from Jamie during her life. Now, with her death, she was still inspiring others to write letters and in doing so find personal meaning. I wonder what Kenneth, whose family had moved away, would have written if he had been with us that day.

Because school had been such an important part of Jamie's life, Laurie and Lambert asked the children and me to be part of her funeral service. We were honored. To prepare, we took turns sharing some of our special memories of Jamie. Then we each wrote down what we wanted to say. I was struck by how much the children remembered, even though it was almost a whole year since we had all been together. Perhaps it was because their experiences had been so meaningful.

Before Jamie's friends could participate in the service, we needed their parents' permission. Our counselors sent a letter to each family, giving the necessary details. The response was overwhelming. All the parents agreed that their children could attend and participate; many said they would be there too. Even parents of children who hadn't known Jamie well asked if they and their children could attend her funeral. I was amazed at how many people loved and admired her. I guess we never really know whom we are affecting.

Jamie's classmates also needed support during this crucial time. Children can react to grief in many ways and need help dealing with their feelings and maintaining their emotional well-being. We therefore contacted HUGS (Help, Understanding, Group Support), a local organization that offers counseling and support for families who have lost a child. A counselor came to work with Jamie's classmates and also offered a session for teachers. Her expertise and understanding were very helpful and greatly appreciated.

Jamie's funeral, on February 11, 1994, was a true celebration of her life and literacy. Hundreds of people attended. Jamie's school photos, albums, and writing, along with photos of her life with her family, were on display. Strangers and loved ones alike found they knew Jamie better after looking at the items her family had so carefully selected and arranged.

The service was very moving. After we sang some of Jamie's favorite hymns, her pastor described what many were feeling:

Her life faced great challenges, and yet she met them with determination and courage. Where many would have given up, she never allowed her handicap to discourage her. . . . Always ready with a smile, even in those last difficult days. Able to joke and laugh even when you knew she had pain. . . . Her faith became her strength and peace. In the last days she gave this faith back to those she loved that they might not fear nor worry over her. Her faith encouraged me and so many others.

Jamie's family and friends then shared personal remembrances. Uncle Chris spoke first and with great eloquence, telling family stories that revealed Jamie's sense of humor, her loving and mischievous sides, and her intelligence. One story stood out:

Jamie's mind was fantastic, it was fast, honest, and intelligent. SHE WASN'T HANDICAPPED—she just couldn't walk. I remember being very angry during Jamie's early therapy when she was given a physical test where blocks had to be stacked up. And this test determined what kind of school Jamie could attend. If she stacked at least four or more blocks, she could attend a regular school. If not, she would be regarded as mentally retarded. Can you even imagine regarding Jamie as mentally retarded?

Well, first strike against Jamie was that the test was administered in the morning; during Jamie's early development and therapy, she was hardly in any mood to do anything in the mornings. Second strike against Jamie was that she couldn't hold her head up to see beyond the second block because of her spine condition.

Well, Jamie did pass the test. And it took Laurie and Lambert and the therapy staff and Jamie herself only a few minutes to convince the person giving the test that Jamie was mentally fine but just physically weak.

Auntie Brenda and I saw Jamie in action at her school class that she attended for three years, and she was a student among everyone else, except for the fact that Jamie was a hot rod on her motorized wheelchair. Jamie was a smart kid—and she knew it.

Chris also told of his appreciation for the positive things that came out of Jamie's illness: "Jamie, we thank you, too, because many of us would not have had the chance to meet at one place if it weren't for visiting you." Thinking of all the people who had come together in Jamie's hospital room, I silently added my thanks as well.

Jarrett spoke next, reading the letter he had written to Jamie for the occasion. I knew how deeply he felt her loss, and I marveled at his composure as he read his good-bye to her. Here are some excerpts:

Hi, Jamie, I know you can hear me and see me, so here it goes. I'm fine and so are Mom and Dad. You probably know, but what I know you don't know is what we are thinking deep inside. I'm fine but sometimes I wonder who is gonna go in the pool with me or who is gonna play a "two player or more" game with me. I really miss a playmate who can't catch me when I do something or cheat.

Many people remind me not to be too sad and to be happy that you're in heaven. But they don't know I'm already doing so. I think they are the ones who can't handle your one-way trip. . . . I bet running is fun. Have you tried tumbling without hands on you yet?

Lambert shared his remembrances and gratitude beautifully, without using notes. Laurie spoke, too, but her words were uncharacteristically few. Then Jamie's classmates and I shared our recollections. Somehow we got through it, in spite of the emotion we were feeling. As I listened to the children, I realized that the simplest words can affect us deeply if they are based on something real; good writing comes from the heart. Their memories of Jamie were real and would stay in their hearts forever. Here is a composite of some of the thoughts they expressed:

We are Jamie's friends from school. We want to celebrate Jamie's goodbye forever. We would like to share our special feelings about Jamie.

Jamie was fun. She played games with us. She used to play jump rope with us. She used to turn the jump rope around and around with us. When the kids were playing Barbies, she gave the boys Kens to play with. She helped Annie build a Barbie house. She made puppet shows with us, like Beverly Hills 90210 *and* The Little Old Lady Who Wasn't Afraid of Anything.

Jamie used to teach us how to read and spell. She helped us read hard words. She helped us to read the thermometer. She let us push her wheelchair, and we used to carry her seat when we went to assemblies.

In first grade, we built a house. Jamie helped us to measure and make the pretend chimney. We made a pretend thing to pump up the fire. She told us to pump up the fire because she couldn't reach it, so we helped her, and we helped her stir the cookie dough for our housewarming party.

Jamie's closest friends had special memories of the happy times they had spent with her:

My name is Jamilee. We shared a lot of secrets and we had fun telling jokes and scary stories. Once we played a joke on the boys at school. We stirred up glitter and glue and spread it all over a little rock. Then we dug a hole where there were plenty of plants and we put the rock in the hole. At recess we pretended we never knew it was there. And the boys said, "Wow, I'd like one piece!"

My name is Mayra. We had fun together. Jamie was smart. Every time when we had a fight, she always helped us solve the problems.

If we had a math problem and got in groups, she said lots of things that helped us think.

My name is Annie. Jamie was nice to everyone. She helped us all with our math. When we had the lemonade stand, she helped us count the money. She helped us measure when we built houses for our mice. One time I went to her house and brought my math stuff and she helped me.

I remember her birthday party. She let us play with anything she got for her birthday.

She let us come with her to church and she invited all of her friends to her house.

My name is Cari. Jamie let us play with her toys. She wasn't selfish. And she said that we didn't have to ask her because she didn't mind.

She liked to invite people to her church.

She was my best friend.

Cari concluded the children's portion of the service this way: "When we were playing with Jamie, she never used to start fights between all of us. So this is time to say good-bye."

Gentle rain, a Hawaiian blessing, fell as Jamie was buried with a purple flower from Jarrett, a family photo, her angel pins, her favorite Barbie doll, and her favorite amethyst rock from our classroom. It was time for all of us to say good-bye.

Reflecting on life and literacy

In the weeks following Jamie's funeral, I visited Laurie as often as I could. Lambert was back at work, Jarrett was back at school, and the relatives had all gone home. This was the most difficult time for her. We talked about Jamie and her life at home and at school. Laurie said that Jamie seemed to find no division between home and school: "They were all life. Jamie *used* reading and writing all the time. Jarrett read because it was assigned; Jamie *wanted* to read. Her reading influenced us, too. We had to read more because she loved to read so much."

One day we talked about the goals that had been set for Jamie in her special-education preschool class: washing her face, tying her shoelaces, holding her spoon and fork with a proper grip, wiping her nose independently, and joining a regular-education class for recess and lunch. We marveled at the changes Jamie had undergone since those days and at how different our goals, and hers, had become. It made me think about the goals we envision for all our students. Should we be asking them to master isolated bits and pieces of information, or should we be fostering more global concepts? Don't the bits and pieces develop, in context and in far more depth, as the larger vision is realized? This debate has raged for a long time in education. My experiences with Jamie helped me know even more clearly where I stood.

We talked that day, too, about the power assessment has to control the course of people's lives. There were so many "what ifs." What if Jamie had not stacked up four blocks during the test her Uncle Chris spoke about? Would her placement really have been decided on the basis of that one performance? And if not, what would have determined her placement? What if our school's administration had not supported a mainstreaming philosophy? We didn't want to think about what might have been. It was too frightening. We in education have such an enormous responsibility to ensure that the assessments we use are appropriate and fair, and that they help, not harm, those entrusted to us.

This was a difficult time for Jamie's classmates, too. I talked with our school counselors and we decided to set up an ongoing, voluntary support group. By mutual agreement with the children, we designated lunchtime every Wednesday as our meeting time. Those who wanted to could eat lunch in my classroom, where we could talk about anything we wished or just enjoy being together. Attendance was not mandatory; the children could come whenever they wanted or needed to, and the counselors would join us whenever possible. I had no intention of being a therapist—I'm not qualified. I simply wanted to be there.

Our support group met for the rest of the school year, somehow needing to maintain our connection as we worked through our feelings. At least ten children always came, though not necessarily the same ones from week to week. Even children Jamie didn't know personally joined us from time to time; she had touched them without knowing it.

What we did varied. Sometimes we talked about school matters and sometimes about personal ones. Sometimes we read books together. The children talked a lot about their memories of Jamie and about how she had influenced them. Many said that they often dreamed about her and that she spoke to them in their dreams. In spite of our sadness, though, we were rarely somber. We laughed a lot, and our laughter was therapeutic. It was important for all of us to feel that we were not dealing with this loss alone.

The children had hoped Laurie would be able to join us occasionally and Laurie said she wanted to, but she found it was just too painful. But she didn't forget Jamie's friends. In April she wrote them a long letter explaining her feelings:

REFLECTING ON LIFE AND LITERACY

I have been thinking of all the kids and especially friends of Jamie there at school, and because I really miss her I cry a lot. Reading the many cards, letters, looking back at pictures, reading her journals from school, remembering our field trips and fun times like the lemonade sale, the secret tree, just a lot of things have made me very sad. I have lots of memories and we are all lucky to have so many of them. Sometimes when I think of Jamie, I laugh a lot too. Sometimes she was very sassy and stubborn. She didn't listen to me all the time, but she always listened to her daddy. I wonder how come?

She really loved school and her classmates a lot. . . . Sometimes when I put things in your recycling bin across the street, I get sad just hearing your voices from the playground. . . . I need to keep busy like how Jamie kept me busy. I need to remember that Jamie wouldn't want me to keep being sad all the time, right?

I plan to take Mr. Panui and Jarrett and maybe her cousins and grandparents to Hawai'i Nature Center and show them the stream, trees, and the hiking trail. She loved nature and wants people to take care of it. . . . She especially loved rainbows, and every time I see one I fondly remember her again. See, there's lots of things that remind me of her. And you guys, her friends, make me think of her all the time.

When I'm finished cleaning Jamie's room, I want to have some of you over to help pick something special of hers that you would want to keep for your special memory like a stuffed animal, or article of clothing, or Barbie. As for her books, I plan on keeping all of them. Her library is so treasured and so many people who come to my house enjoy reading the books. Maybe you might consider asking for books for gifts instead of toys. There was a letter that Jamie wrote when she knew she was dying, and she didn't want any toys at all. At the hospital, she just wanted people to read to her many books because all she had to do was listen. People around her loved the stories, too. She loved to read to them, but when her eyes got tired, she asked others to do it for her.

Anyway, just because I don't see you guys at the school yet or call you, doesn't mean I don't think of you. In fact, I love all of you very much and think of you often. I know we all miss Jamie very much. But it's okay to cry. I know it will take time, but we'll be strong like before. . . . I know she remembers all of you and you all will never stop being friends. You still have me, Mr. Panui, and, of course, Jarrett. Call me if you want.

I thought often in those days about my own "what ifs": What if Jamie had been accepted at her neighborhood school and I had never met her? What if I had not taken the risk of curricular change? What if circumstances had not enabled us to have three years together? Life takes mysterious paths, and we can never know why. All we can do is embrace it and give it the best we have and be thankful for all the wondrous things it gives back to us.

Epilogue

Life does go on. Laurie once mentioned a quotation to me that reminded her of Jamie: "Courage is resistance to fear, mastery of fear—not absence of fear" (Clemens 1894). Somehow we all found that courage and prepared ourselves to go on without Jamie. But it didn't happen quite that way. So many things have happened, and are still happening, that I know Jamie is still with us and that the fruits of her literacy continue to grow.

Laurie and Lambert have read Jamie's journals and other writing over and over. They find a great deal of comfort there: "It's more precious than other things." They now pay even closer attention to what and how Jamie wrote, and new aspects of her personality are constantly revealed. Jamie's writing keeps her alive.

Jarrett has become the guardian of Jamie's rock collection, learning more about rocks as he cares for it lovingly. He is still very interested in science and was able to attend space camp last year. He has also developed a renewed interest in reading and writing and has found, to his surprise, that he is a very competent writer. In fact, an article he wrote as a seventh grader was included in a book published by his school, and he was one of only three students younger than high school age to be so honored.

Laurie's brother Monty was inspired to write several collections of poems about Jamie, which he illustrated and bound most artistically and gave to her family. He feels Jamie's presence constantly.

Monty, his wife, Yoshiko, and their five-year-old daughter, Tracy, recently moved back to Hawai'i and are living next door to Jamie's family. Tracy was only a year old the one time she met Jamie. But when she returned to the Panui's house, she was immediately drawn to Jamie's books. She loves looking at them and having them read to her over and over again. But a most extraordinary event occurred the day Tracy asked for a piece of paper, wrote something on it, and placed it by a photo of

Jamie. She said it was a letter to Jamie! In Japan, she had never expressed an interest in writing, nor had her Hawai'i relatives ever spoken to her about Jamie's literacy experiences. No one knows what motivated her to write that letter, but she has written dozens more since, in both Japanese (her first language) and English, and has taped them all over the door to Jamie's room. She dictated a message for her mother to write on one of the envelopes: "I'm lonely because you died. If you live now, I'm so happy." She continues to write and has asked for pens, pencils, and notepads for Christmas—no toys.

Other family members know and benefit from Jamie's presence, too. One day, Grandma Lo was telling her coworkers about a book that Jamie had especially loved, *Someday Heaven*. They wanted to see the book, so Ms. Lo brought it to work the next day and showed it to them during their lunch hour. Many of the women were second-language learners who could not read English, so they asked Ms. Lo to read it to them. They listened, enthralled, as they ate. They were disappointed that lunchtime was over before the story was finished, and asked to have it continued the next day. Because it was quite a long book and they discussed it as they went along, it took several days to finish. By the end of the story the women were hooked, and they asked Ms. Lo to bring more of Jamie's favorite books. That was the beginning of a new tradition, Grandma Lo's lunchtime story hour. It has been a blessing for her as well as for her coworkers. She feels a renewed closeness to Jamie as she rediscovers the stories that Jamie loved so dearly and reaches out to others in the process.

Recently, Lambert's mother had major surgery and found herself helplessly hooked to a ventilator like the one Jamie had endured, cut off from communication with others in the same way. But this time Laurie and Lambert knew what to do. They brought Grandma Panui paper and pens so she could make her needs known and increase her comfort and speed her recovery. Jamie would have been happy to know how much she had helped her grandma!

Laurie talked about going back to work later in the year, but the clerical jobs she'd done before weren't much of a motivation. She told me many times that she wished she could find work that involved teaching adults to read or helping them learn more about reading and writing with their children. She wanted other parents to experience the joy of sharing in their children's developing literacy, but she knew that many did not have the background to do so.

Laurie's dream was a worthy one, but nothing came of it. The job she envisioned didn't seem to exist, at least not in our area. She offered her services to various volunteer literacy groups, but most of them told her that they would accept only certified teachers. Others never responded to her inquiries. She finally tried some temporary office jobs just to keep busy, but none of them was fulfilling.

In May 1995, I served on a committee to plan our school's literacy focus for the following year. One of our major goals was to increase the involvement of families in their children's education, with particular emphasis on early literacy efforts. After a brainstorming session, backed up with special funding, we created the new part-time position of family literacy coordinator; this person would work with parents and teachers toward achieving our goals. The committee wanted a parent, not a teacher, for this position, reasoning that parents might find another parent less intimidating to work with. They also needed someone who had the necessary expertise, who was able to work with people, and who loved reading.

How amazing life's coincidences are—or are they coincidences? As soon as the job description was written, I knew whom it had been written for. This was the job of Laurie's dreams, and she was the ideal person to fill it. She was hired to begin working in September 1995.

Unfortunately, Laurie found that it was just too soon for her to do this sort of work, especially at Jamie's school, with its many painful memories. Although she was doing an outstanding job, she reluctantly resigned in early 1996. She has since found a position that is easier for her to deal with emotionally yet still enables her to help others. She currently works for our state department of human services, helping disabled people acquire jobs. She's finding it fulfilling, especially as she remembers Jamie's deep concern for society's treatment of those with disabilities. She is also taking courses at a community college because, as she says, "I want to keep learning." I know she will continue the journey.

Jamie's friends were able to go on, too, and are now active, typically sociable sixth graders. But Jamie is still part of their lives, and they still keep in touch with her family. Some borrow and reread Jamie's books; some still write letters to her. At their request, we've met several times at the Panui's house, for what we have termed our "'Ohana reunions." These have been joyful occasions, filled with laughter and good feelings. Even though Laurie found the school setting too difficult, she and Lambert are happy to have Jamie's friends visit their home. It's reassuring to see how resilient the children are and to know for ourselves that they are okay but that they still remember. In time, Jamie's physical image may fade from their memory, but what is important will remain. "It is only with the heart that one can see rightly; what is essential is invisible to the eye" (Saint-Exupéry 1943).

Jamie's story brings up many issues for me, issues I think about a lot. Foremost are two questions: What is literacy for? What's important in life?

When I spoke at Jamie's funeral, I said, "It was a privilege to be Jamie's teacher; but truthfully, she was my teacher even more. She helped me see more clearly what teaching and learning should be all about." I feel this even more strongly now, almost three years later. Literacy is not about skills and test scores; it's about enriching our lives. Jamie's eight years were rich, and her literacy and life are continuing to touch others.

Life is uncertain; we never know what will happen. Hearing Jamie's story, Joe Tobin, one of my University of Hawai'i professors, said, "There's not necessarily a long-range payoff for what we ask our students to do or for what they learn. What counts is a minute-to-minute life of meaning." Jamie's life had that meaning. Although her death might cause us to see this meaning more clearly, it was her life that generated the meaning in the first place. At Jamie's funeral, the HUGS counselor said, "This little girl lived life to the fullest." I believe that Jamie's love and ownership of literature and writing—the *power* of her literacy—helped her do that. I only wish we could help all our students find that same power for themselves, whether they have eight years or 108 years to exercise it in. That's the greatest gift we could give them.

When I think of Jamie, I see her zipping into the classroom in her wheelchair, with the biggest and brightest smile on her face; I see her sharing, talking, and laughing with her school 'Ohana; and I hear her eager voice saying, "I can't wait until I read the next chapter of this book" or "I'm going to write a new book today." And I think of the words she wrote during her stay at Shriners Hospital, words that describe perfectly how she saw herself and how she would wish us to remember her:

MY AUTOBIOGRAPHY

Hi! My name is Jamie Panui. I am eight years old and have two kinds of wheelchairs. One is motorized and the other is a manual wheelchair. I like to play and make new friends. I like to eat french fries and all kinds of stuff. I like to make people happy. I like to play "school" with my brother at home. My mom's name is Laurie and my dad's name is Lambert and my brother's name is Jarrett. My brother is eleven and we like to play together. I like to spend time with my mom and my dad and my whole family.

It's a lot of fun to go to school. I have a lot of friends at school. Their names are Cari, Mayra, Annie, and Jamilee. They are very good friends and they are very helpful to me. I try to help them, too.

When I was born
In the world of man
I knew I was loved
When mom touched my hand.
When I was two
A cute darling was I
I knew I was loved
When dad heard my cry.
When I was four
A loving family were we
I knew I was loved
When my brother kissed me.
When I was six
I came to learn quite quick
I knew I was loved
Even though I was sick.
When I was eight
I drank from the lord's cup
I knew I was loved
So I never gave up.

MONTGOMERY (MONTY) LO

References

Anderson, Richard, Elfrieda Hiebert, Judith Scott, and Ian Wilkinson. 1985. *Becoming a Nation of Readers*. Washington: U.S. Department of Education, National Institute of Education.

Bakhtin, Mikhail. 1981. "Discourse in the Novel." In M. Holmquist, ed., *The Dialogic Imagination: Four Essays by M. M. Bakhtin*. Austin, TX: University of Texas Press.

Bissex, Glenda. 1980. *GNYS AT WRK: A Child Learns to Write and Read*. Cambridge: Harvard University Press.

Cazden, Courtney. 1981. "Language and Learning to Read." In C. Cazden, ed., *Language in Early Childhood Education*. Washington, DC: The National Association for the Education of Young Children.

Clemens, Samuel. 1894 (1981). *Pudd'nhead Wilson*. New York: Bantam.

Dewey, John. 1916. *Democracy and Education: An Introduction to the Philosophy of Education*. New York: Macmillan.

Ferreiro, Emilia, and Ana Teberosky. 1982. *Literacy Before Schooling*. Portsmouth, NH: Heinemann.

Goodman, Yetta, ed. 1986. *How Children Construct Literacy: Piagetian Perspectives*. Newark, DE: International Reading Association.

Harste, Jerome, Kathy Short, and Carolyn Burke. 1988. *Creating Classrooms for Authors*. Portsmouth, NH: Heinemann.

Kamii, Constance, Maryann Manning, and Gary Manning, eds. 1991. *Early Literacy: A Constructivist Foundation for Whole Language*. Washington, DC: National Education Association.

Lewis, Rena, and Donald Doorlag. 1987. *Teaching Special Students in the Mainstream*. Columbus, OH: Merrill.

Madden, Nancy, and Robert Slavin. 1983. "Mainstreaming Students with Mild Handicaps: Academic and Social Outcomes." *Review of Educational Research* 53, 519–69.

Peterson, Ralph, and Maryann Eeds. 1990. *Grand Conversations*. Richmond Hill, Ontario: Scholastic.

Rosenblatt, Louise. 1978. *The Reader, the Text, the Poem: The Transactional Theory of the Literary Work*. Carbondale, IL: Southern Illinois University Press.

Saint-Exupéry, Antoine de. 1943. *The Little Prince*. New York: Harcourt, Brace.

Short, Kathy, and Kathryn Pierce. 1990. *Talking About Books: Creating Literate Communities*. Portsmouth, NH: Heinemann.

Turnbull, Ann, and Rutherford Turnbull. 1986. *Families, Professionals, and Exceptionality: A Special Partnership*. Columbus, OH: Merrill.

Wells, Gordon. 1990. "Talk About Text: Where Literacy Is Learned and Taught." *Curriculum Inquiry* 20, 369–405.

Bibliography of children's books

About Handicaps. Sara Stein. New York: Walker, 1974.

Angus and the Cat. Marjorie Flack. New York: Doubleday, 1931.

Ant Cities. Arthur Dorros. New York: HarperCollins, 1987.

Are You My Mother? Philip Eastman. New York: Random House, 1966.

Barry: The Bravest St. Bernard. Lynn Hall. New York: Random House, 1992.

The Boxcar Children. Gertrude Warner. Chicago: Albert Whitman, 1953.

Bunnicula. Deborah Howe and James Howe. New York: Atheneum, 1979.

A Cache of Jewels. Ruth Heller. New York: Putnam, 1989.

Chang's Shell. Ralph Robinett, Paul Bell, and Pauline Rojas. Lexington, MA: D. C. Heath, 1970.

Charlotte's Web. E. B. White. New York: HarperCollins, 1952.

Copycat. Ruth Brook. New York: Dutton Child Books, 1994.

Creature Features. David Drew. Australia: Thomas Nelson, 1988.

Elizabeth's Super-Selling Lemonade. Molly Mia Steward. New York: Bantam Books, 1990.

Good Neighbors. Diane Massie. Middletown, CT: American Education Publishers, 1972.

Green Eggs and Ham. Theodore Geisel. New York: Random House, 1960.

Henny Penny. Paul Galdone. Boston: Clarion, 1984.

Home for a Puppy. Sharon Gordon. Mahwah, NJ: Troll, 1988.

How to Deal with Friends. Richard Powell. Mahwah, NJ: Watermill Press, 1990.

Leo, the Late Bloomer. Robert Kraus. New York: Windmill, 1971.

The Little Old Lady Who Wasn't Afraid of Anything. Linda Williams. New York: Harper and Row, 1986.

Mickey's Magnet. Franklyn Branley. New York: Crowell, 1956.

Mike's New Bike. Rose Greydanus. Mahwah, NJ: Troll, 1980.

Moon Mouse. Adelaide Holl. New York: Random House, 1969.

Morris Goes to School. Bernard Wiseman. New York: Harper and Row, 1970.

My Dog and the Knock Knock Mystery. David Adler. New York: Holiday House, 1985.

My Father's Dragon. Ruth Gannett. New York: Knopf, 1948.

My Grandma Has Black Hair. Mary Hoffman. New York: Doubleday, 1988.

The New Baby. Mercer Mayer. Racine, WI: Western, 1985.

No Elephants Allowed. Deborah Robison. Boston: Houghton Mifflin, 1981.

One Fish, Two Fish, Red Fish, Blue Fish. Theodore Geisel. New York: Random House, 1960.

Over in the Meadow. John Langstaff. San Diego: Harcourt Brace, 1992.

Petunia. Roger Duvoisin. New York: Knopf, 1950.

Play It Again, Rosie. Ruth Brook. Mahwah, NJ: Troll, 1988.

Road Robber. Joy Cowley. San Diego: The Wright Group, 1988.

Solomon the Rusty Nail. William Steig. New York: Farrar, Straus and Giroux, 1987.

Someday Heaven. Larry Libby. Sisters, OR: Questar, 1993.

Someone Special, Just Like You. Tricia Brown. New York: Holt, 1984.

Springtime Surprises. Judith Conaway. Mahwah, NJ: Troll, 1986.

Swimmy. Leo Lionni. New York: Knopf, 1963.

The Three Little Hawaiian Pigs and the Magic Shark. Donivee Laird. Honolulu: Barnaby Books, 1981.

When I Was Young in the Mountains. Cynthia Rylant. New York: Dutton, 1982.